I0185765

THE WEIGHT OF IT ALL

a book about gloriously heavy things

Jacob Hale

Published 2023
ISBN: 979-8-9880296-0-1

In memory and honor of my beloved.

Steadfast in faithfulness and joy, delightful beyond measure, beautiful as the sun.

Till we see each other in the garden to come.

Table of Contents

Introduction

The Preacher sought to find words of delight,
and uprightly he wrote words of truth...
Of making many books there is no end,
and much study is a weariness of the flesh.
-Ecclesiastes 12:10, 12

What am I Doing?

What am I doing? What thoughts do I think I have that could be of any worth or value, or at least enough value to be distributed to others in pages of valuable paper? What do I think I can add to any conversation beyond what is already written in inestimable volumes? I don't know the answer fully. I just know that things have been percolating in my mind and heart and soul for some time.

After finishing the first draft I gave this book to my wife to read. After reading it she asked me, "How would you describe your book? Would it be a memoir? A manifesto? What?" I pondered this for a moment before half jokingly saying that it was, "A screaming into the wind." That's what it feels like for me at times, but this joke falls short of really describing what this is. Let's begin with discussing what this book is not. This book is not a theological tome, though there is theology in, with, under, and throughout. This book is not a memoir or autobiography, though you will learn a lot about me and my life throughout it. This book is not a practical handbook for some aspect of the Christian life, though there are practical charges and implications. This book is not a biblical commentary, though the Bible is quoted throughout.

This book is a meditation, a prayer, and a benediction. Or, a medipraydiction if you will allow me some silliness (if this silliness annoys you, I have bad news about the rest of the contents of this book). It is a meditation because it is a dwelling on certain things. An attempt to allow some things to sit in my mind and to allow my mind to sit in some things. A prayer because it is a cry to God for understanding, wisdom, change, and more. An attempt to seek divine help under the weight of these things. And a benediction because it is, hopefully, a good word for me and for you. A word that will bless and bring delight. And in these things, ultimately, it is a catharsis for me. A release of things too heavy and weighty for my soul and mind.

The Weight of It All

Sometimes when I drink soda while sitting the gas gets trapped and can't make its way out. I feel it like a big balloon in my chest. I stand and straighten and all that gas comes ripping out in a smelly, cacophonous roar that offends or impresses my wife, depending on the mood she's in. That's what this book feels like. The output of thoughts and feelings and things too deep for words that have been building in my soul's chest. And now they have exploded out of my soul into words, into a book, into something that may be rank, may offend, but maybe, just maybe, will delight and inspire.

Sometimes I get overwhelmed by everything. Not in the sense that I'm too busy or too unorganized, though that happens. No, I get overwhelmed by the sheer size and sheer reality of everything. Have you ever actually seen a tree? Have you really studied one, following all the splitting branches and twigs like frozen lightning. Trees frighten me sometimes. They're everywhere and they're big and they're real. You can climb one if you want. Or make a fire. There are other things that are real. Trees, puppies, eagles, minks, waterfalls, fathers, mothers, loves, bread, wine, grace, all these things exist, and not only do they exist but they have existed and come from somewhere and are going somewhere.

What would it be to truly know anything? Try to wrap your mind around an ant. Find one in your yard. See it. Hold it in your mind. Follow it. See all the hidden paths it takes to the various foods it eats. Find out which ants it likes, which ants it hates. Find out its father, its mother. How did its colony get here? Were they outcasts from some ancient civil war a few months ago or were they a colony planted in hopes of expanding territory? Where did it come from? Where is it going? Feel the futility of it. It's all too much. We can't fully know a single ant.

What about you, reader? Where are you? A nice chair or couch I hope. Maybe with a nice beverage to enjoy while reading. What brought you here? What hidden paths shaped your life? Who was your father, your grandfather, your great grandfather, your great great grandfather? What places did they go, what things did they see that molded them and changed them and led to you and who you are? Who will your children be?

There's so much in this world and in my life, and at times when I try to hold it all in my mind I feel overwhelmed. Like the ant, trying to lift a planet made of granite. Scrambling for any purchase, any leverage, any way to hold the weight of it all without being crushed. I search for some way to explain, some way to express, some way to get a kind of relief from the pressure. Sometimes I burp. Sometimes I cry. Sometimes I sing. And sometimes, when the need is too great, I write. Trying to find just the right words that can convey something beyond words.

That's what this book is, my dealing with heavy things. Not necessarily dark and dreary heavy, though there are some. Heavy in the way glory is heavy. Thick, meaningful, big, and real. When was the last time you felt the reality of something? Loss is real. Pain is real. But so is love and the giggling of a child and the gleeful damage puppies can do in an unlocked crawl space.

My hope in this smelly, unpolished, belch of a book is that I can help myself and you feel the reality of God's reality more fully. That I can write something, anything, that even begins to capture the sheer beauty and terror and size of the things that are all around us. That together we can feel the weight of all these things and see the glory behind them more clearly. And give myself some relief.

Chapter 1

Existence

God of our fathers, Whose almighty hand
Leads forth in beauty all the starry band
Of shining worlds in splendor thro' the skies,
Our grateful songs before Thy throne arise.
Thy love divine hath led us in the past;
In this free land by Thee our lot is cast;
Be Thou our ruler, guardian, guide and stay,
Thy word our law, Thy paths our chosen way.
-from God of Our Fathers

Dust and Spirit

C.S. Lewis is said to have said, "You don't have a soul. You are a soul. You have a body." This is wrong. Both in that he never said it and in that it's wrong. You are a body. You are a soul. "Then the Lord God formed the man of dust from the ground and breathed into his nostrils the breath of life, and the man became a living creature." Now we're getting somewhere. Dust of the earth. Not star dust like all those lame self-important Facebook posts talk about. Dust dust. The kind you get yelled at for tracking into the kitchen. The kind that belongs under fingernails. The kind you'll return to one day.

Go to a graveyard some time. Stare at all the names etched in granite. Stare at the graves. Behold! Dust. That shouldn't scare you though. There are a lot of perks to this whole "life" thing. Food is nice. Sex is great. Smells are hit or miss but even the bad ones can make for good stories.

But that's just half the story. You are dust, yes, but dust that has the very breath of God moving through it. Despite what the self important prophets of atheism and their edgy acolytes may think, we're not simply physical beings. (For more information on these people see chapter 5). You are breath. You are spirit. You have as part of your very nature a small echo of God's own nature. He has made us, not like animals, but like Him, in His own image. The ancient Greeks looked at the night sky and saw gods in the stars. Dust and sacred together. I've seen the stars. They lifted their gaze too high.

What does it mean to be, to exist? Famous philosopher Rene Descartes said that he thought and therefore he was. Is existence consciousness then? Is it being aware? What's the answer? The answer is easy, despite centuries of philosophers muddying the waters. Existence is being. Existing is existing. C'est la vie. It is what it is. You know what it means to exist in a general sense *because you're doing it right now*. I'm not interested in philosophical ponderings that lead nowhere with no concrete answers. I want answers that mean something. I want answers that touch the mud and blood of our lives and leave us with hard won precious truths we can latch onto in the storms of life. For those kinds of questions and answers philosophers are little help. Philosophy is a help, but philosophers too often seek to answer the easiest questions in the most confusing way. Existence is easy to define because you experience it now. Thanks Descartes but we're good here.

So what's the important question then? What's the hard question? The best question you can ask about your own existence is what does it mean to be dust and spirit? What does it mean to be a human being, made from the earth and heaven? What does it mean to be you?

The Line of Dust

Most of our problems, we're told, come from our parents. They didn't love us enough, didn't scold us enough, didn't breastfeed, did breastfeed, didn't teach us right. We can blame a lot on our parents, but you exist. You. You have agency and will. No matter their faults or efforts, we are our own beings and make our own choices. You are more than the sum of your parents' mistakes or triumphs. And yet there is some value to considering where we come from. The way in which we came into the world and the stories that helped to shape our own.

The first poem I ever wrote was about my hands. In God's gracious providence the poem is long lost, but don't get too excited, there are other poems later. I remember standing on my porch in college looking at my hands. My father had just given me a jacket that he had worn for years as a gift. My hands seemed odd poking out of the cuffs. Strangers in a strange land. The moment pressed and I began to feel the weight of it. My father, my father's father, my children one day. And so I wrote about how my hands are so unlike my dad's. So unscarred, so uncalloused, so different. I wondered if they would be like his hands one day. If time and age would mold them and change them. If there would be a time I'd look only to find my hands gone and my father's hands in their place. Would I have a son to give a jacket to then?

You come from somewhere. The dust that makes up part of you began in another person. A person with thoughts and dreams and dust and breath and an existence of their own. And they came from someone and on and on and on. What do you know of your great-great-great-great grandfather? I don't know much, but I know mine was a man named Billy Hale. Billy came to America for a better life and settled on a mountain right on the Tennessee-Alabama border. I know he had 21 children. I know he was a bit of a scoundrel. I know he ate. I know he dreamed. I know he existed. I know I owe my own existence in part to him.

I know my grandfather and father better. My grandfather is a primitive Baptist preacher. He's fiery and sharp, even in old age. I spent time with him and a camera. Preserving his own story of life and love and grace for myself and my children and maybe one day my great grandchildren. He tells a story of my father and his two brothers when they were young and wonderfully foolish. They decided to play cowboys and Indians. My father somehow ended up as the "Indian" and the other two "cowboys" decided to hang him. My uncle Max had the knowledge of how to tie a real noose and none of the wisdom requisite for that knowledge. My grandfather caught them as my father stood on a chair with a noose around his neck. A little later and maybe you wouldn't have this book in your hands.

That's a fun story but it is not a rare one. Life is full of near deaths. Every time you get in a car you roll the dice. Every time you breathe you take a chance there's some airborne disease that will end you. Every time you step outside you're risking a meteor striking you. Aneurysms lurk in every shadow. Every moment is fraught with danger. But danger isn't the only thing you need to watch out for. Chance is a vicious killer too.

My father met my mother working at a factory that makes airplane windshields. They hit it off and got married and here I and my sister are. My father told me once that he wished he'd gone into government work instead of working at the factory. He was young and there was an opportunity for a cushy government job that would have paid more and been easier on his body. He had a contact who had assured him that he would get the position. But then, chance. A new president, a new policy, a freeze on government hiring. My father was left without a job and began working at the factory. He tells me the story on his back porch and I smile and tell him, "Well, I suppose I have to thank that president the next time I see him." I suppose whoever would've been here if chance had moved differently isn't pleased, but that's his problem.

Chance, danger, desires, needs, all these shape our dusty existence and leave lasting impacts that not only mold us but shape the course of generations and generations of people. Remember that the next time you get a flat tire.

What is existence? What does it mean to be? In part the answer to that question is to look beyond your own existence. To cast your eyes to the line of dust extending behind and before you. To feel the weight of your place in this thing called reality and see where you came from and try to see what is coming. You didn't pop into existence out of nothing. The world didn't begin when you first gained consciousness. None of us exist on our own.

You might have some push back now. "My parents suck. I don't know my parents. I don't know how to learn these things." I understand your concerns. Parents can suck. They can harm and hurt deeper than almost anyone else. People can lose their history. The line can be obscured. But I'm not saying you have to learn funny stories or cool facts. I'm not saying that you need to learn your genealogy or anything like that. This is deeper and bigger than that. I'm saying that we have to stop thinking about ourselves as self-contained realities. You are not the star of this show. You are not the protagonist of existence. You came into reality *in media res* and you will leave this world in the same way.

In part, to know what it is to exist is to recognize that other people exist and you owe your own existence to thousands and thousands of other's hungers and missed opportunities and near deaths. It is to see the line of dust behind and before you.

The Chain of Dust

But the idea of a line implies a continuity that isn't really there. It doesn't capture the beginnings and endings adequately. A chain is a better analogy. Beginnings and endings overlapping with what came before and what will remain after. Billy Hale had his end. Jacob Hale will too. One day, my child will have his or her end. And so will you. Dust to dust.

When the world was young and the stars first shone down on this spinning ball a line might have been the better analogy. Then there were no ends. No death. Our first parents had been made from dust and had no prospects of returning to it. And then a dragon and a fruit. Our parents decided to define good and evil for themselves and rebelled. And God, ever faithful and true to His word, kept His promise. In the day you eat of it you shall surely die. Death, that curse, entered the world. Dust to dust. We are made from dust and returning to it soon. Sooner than any of us might like to think. What does it mean to exist as dust? For one thing it means that we have beginnings. We have births. We come from somewhere and exist because of others' decisions and choices. That's part one. Time for part two.

You will die. Take a moment. Breathe that truth in. Let it sink into your flesh, into your bones, into your marrow. Into your very soul. You will die. There is no escaping this. There is no bargain you can make. There is no game of chess or dice you can win. There is no potion or pill you can take. You are helpless against this enemy. No matter how righteous you are, no matter how healthy you are, no matter how rich you are, no matter how powerful you are, you will die.

You need to dwell on this for a moment because we are so slow to believe this. We all are quick to assume that reality began when we did and that we will endure as long as it does. When we're young we feel that we are invincible. Nothing can hurt us or stop us. Eighty or ninety years seems like an eternity. As we age we learn the folly of such thoughts. We get cancers and suffer loss. The years go faster and faster and faster. But still that tendency to forget rears its head, though it adapts to our wisdom. Instead of feeling immortal we simply don't think about death. We try to push it away. We try to forget. We fill our minds and time with anything and everything we can to drown out the howls of that grim wolf. Whether young and ignorant or old and stubborn, we don't feel the reality of our impending deaths.

But we are dust and part of what it means to exist as dust is to return to that dust. To live as dust is to live with the understanding that you will die. The chain link starts and ends.

But this isn't to say that you need to be fixated on death. When we really begin to grapple with our end, we can react in many poor ways. We can romanticize death like a teenage girl in love with the idea of a Romeo and Juliet scenario. We can idolize death with suicidal or nihilistic thoughts. Death becomes a god in some ways. But while death is inescapable it is by no means almighty.

The best way to think of death is in Biblical categories. What is death in the Bible? Why do our links in the chain end? Death is the fulfillment of a promise. Death is the reward for breaking God's command. Our first parents Adam and Eve were told if they ate of the fruit of the tree of the knowledge of good and evil then they would die. And they did eat, and they did die, and we will too. God was faithful to keep His promise and cursed them with death for their sin. And now as we all sin, we all die. Death is a curse for our rebellion. It's a reminder of our sin and a reminder of God's faithfulness.

But death is not only a curse, it is a blessing in a few ways. I remember many of my sins. I remember how I hurt my mother when I was young. She wouldn't let me stay up late and play video games and so I filled an entire sheet of paper with the same sentence over and over again. "Mama's mean." She only had my best interests at heart. She loved me dearly and wanted me to be healthy and get sleep. But I was selfish and prideful. I wanted my way. And so I hurt her. And that memory haunts me. It's been many years since that incident but it still eats at me. I still regret doing that. It breaks my heart to think of how my mom must have felt. But you might say, you were a child and that's not really that bad. I remember more heinous sins too. I remember lies and anger and selfishness and lust and slander and covetousness and more.

Sometimes I lie awake thinking of all my regrets and all the things I've done poorly. They chase sleep from me. I'm only 30 years old. I'm not that old. Lord willing, I have many more decades of regrets and mental scars and sins to look forward to. I hope to grow in holiness, but I also know that I will fail again. Think of all the sins and regrets and sadness and embarrassment that piles up like so much garbage in a landfill just in 30 years. Imagine how you'll feel at 70. Imagine how you'd feel at 400, 900, 24028, and more. Eternity as a sinner would be unbearable. Eternity in a fallen and cursed world would be more hell than heaven.

And so, the Lord curses us with a cure for sin and regret and an escape from this fallen world through death. Even in His judgments and curses, the Lord is kind. But death is a blessing in another way too. Death not only brings an end to our sin and suffering, it gives a unique pleasure to life. It allows us to live for things that are beyond ourselves. It allows us to sacrifice and live for others.

Come with me for a tour of my yard for a minute. Here is my garden, getting ready for spring planting. Here are my apple trees, still young and nowhere near producing apples. Here is my chicken coop, there are a few eggs in there if you're hungry. And here is a particular joy of mine, a huge oak tree. Every yard needs a good oak tree with spreading limbs offering shade and dropping sweet acorns for pigs and puppies to chew on and children to collect like treasures. Unfortunately if your house is newer or in a newer development you probably don't have the luxury of a beautiful ancient oak tree. Most landscapists prefer maples. Now maples are a good tree, but they don't hold a candle to the majesty of an oak. But maples grow fast. An average maple tree will take 10 years to grow to maturity. An oak will take 30-40 years to grow to maturity. Using my best estimations my glorious oak tree is about 60-70 years old. I could plant another oak today and I'd be in my seventies before it was full grown. I'd be near a hundred before it could match the oak I currently have. Though, in all likelihood, I wouldn't be near a hundred years old. The average man in America lives until 78, so in all likelihood I'd be dead for 20 years or more.

That's probably more tree-talk than you were expecting and there's some more talk of trees later, but the point is why would any adult ever plant an oak tree if they'd be too old or too dead to ever really enjoy it? Why do parents try to build a household, a business, a bank account that will outlast them when it will outlast them? Why does anyone go off to fight in wars when it means they could lose the one precious life they have? Why does anyone become a firefighter or police officer or any dangerous occupation when it means you could die? We only get one life to live so why would we ever do anything that isn't immediately beneficial to our one life? Why risk?

Death is inevitable. Death is coming. Death is already on its way. Cancer is growing in hidden recesses of your body. The drunk driver is already on the road to meet you on your way to the store. Your heart is already growing tired and weak and stressed. Your link in the chain will end. But the beautiful thing is that there can be another link after you. You don't have to end and end. You can end and continue on by being the start of something new. A new story. A new life. New loves and new joys and new trees. Those who come after you can sit in the shade of the oaks you plant and their children can gather up the acorns. I don't know who planted the mighty oak I enjoy today. But I thank God for them and whatever led them to plant that tree and give me pleasure and an illustration.

Death allows us to live for more than ourselves. To see past the limitations of our own dust and see those who will come after us and do things now for them. To sacrifice our time and energy and wealth and yes, even our lives for those who may never remember us but will owe their place in God's story to our actions. What does it mean to be dust? It means to know that we begin and we will end, and yet our beginnings and endings are not The Beginning and not The End. Just the next link in the chain.

The Line of Breath

I sit on my porch writing now. It's late and one of my puppies cuddles under my chair. I give her a pet and she stirs and gently licks my hand. Louise here has a father and mother. Her mother is a black lab, born for play and cuddles. Her father is an Anatolian shepherd, born for guarding livestock and working. She has a line just like me. She will die one day, just like me. What separates us? What makes you and her different? What does it mean to exist as not only dust but breath? What does it mean to have God's own image as part of my very nature?

Louise doesn't have existential crises like we do. I've never seen her worrying about what it means to be a dog. In fact, most animals have no need for philosophy in general. You don't find a Plato among squirrels arguing about the ideal nuttiness of a nut. You don't find a Nietzsche among the ants promoting the idea of an überameise. No, there's something uniquely human in our struggle to know what it means to be us. It's a little ironic really. What makes us think and worry and philosophize? How are we different from animals?

Let us return again to the beginning, though not all the way back. Just a few days into the creation of the world. God has been busy establishing the pillars of the earth and populating the seas, land, and air with creepy crawlies, bison, puppies, hawks, chickens, tuna, guppies, leviathans, and behemoths. And to top all of it, to crown His creation He makes humanity from the dust and from His own breath. And then, God gives them dominion over everything else. They are to rule the earth as God's stewards. Why? What is happening here? God created humanity not only as physical beings like the animals and not only as spiritual beings like Himself and the angels but as physical and spiritual beings. We exist at the intersection of physical and spiritual reality. We are emissaries of both to the other. And so, we rule over the earth as God's stewards because we are the representatives of the spiritual King. And we care for and contend for the earth because we are of the earth.

We are spiritual beings. But just as the taste of the fruit ruined our physical reality with the rot of death and thorns, so too does it ruin our spiritual reality. No longer are we in harmony with our Father. No longer do our souls know peace. Instead we are blinded, calloused, hardened, even dead to the spiritual reality of our being. We live as incomplete people in our rebellion. And everyone feels this. Oh you may lie enough to yourself to make yourself believe you don't. Or you might take up all sorts of various hobbies, licit or otherwise, to numb that reality, but we all feel that no matter how well our physical reality is going there is something else that is wrong. Something else is out of line. Something else is missing.

Our spiritual dimension is ruined but not removed. And so, we're all searching for something without quite knowing what it is. We write and paint and worry and pontificate. Philosophers try to crack the nut with a variety of questions (ideally with no concrete answers). What is the meaning of life? What are we here for? What is meaningful? But in the end, our searching is a symptom of our spiritual spoilage.

To be made from dust and breath means that we are made for more than this earth. We are of the earth but eternity is in our hearts and we feel the need for something more. God graced us with a spirit and body. Heaven and earth, divine and dust, in one. You carry within you an echo of God's own nature and personality.

You are made like God. You share in His being in a sense. You love, you hate, you rejoice, you get angry, you sing, you work, you care, you move, you think, and so much more. The Greeks made gods in their image. Brutish, petty, horny, and so very human. But in this as in many things, they were all mixed up. What makes us different from animals is that we share in the divine nature, even though it is decayed and decaying due to sin.

So why do we struggle with all these questions? Why do we search for meaning and purpose? Because we were made to be little mirrors reflecting back the character and nature of God to the world. To follow Him. To live like Him. To be like Him. We all intrinsically know this. We feel it in the bones of our soul. We simply suppress the truth in our unrighteousness. We turn our backs on the one who made us different from the rest of creation and worship images resembling created things or even parts of creation itself.

We follow false gods made in our own image. We worship money and success and food and more. Like the Greeks we get it all mixed up.

But it doesn't have to be this way of course. What does it mean to be YOU? In part, existence is our physical reality in the past, present, and future. Our link on the chain of dust. That's half of it. The other half is the spiritual reality. The fact that you have a spirit that is made to reflect and worship God and can never die. Your soul is meant to find its home in the infinite God for all eternity. Your soul can never die but will exist forever. We are made for eternity and infinity. Is it any wonder then that this world and our lives are never enough? Is it any wonder then that we feel the need for something more and something grander than the mundane? And when we embrace this truth and return to the Father of spirits we find life and find it abundantly. Life as it was meant to be. Physical and spiritual. Mundane and glorious. Earth and Heaven. Dust and breath joined together, supporting each other, and informing each other.

But what about that pesky little problem of death? You're going to die. How does that factor into this? Will we simply be spirits forever while our physical form is left behind to rot? That's how many envision eternity. Clouds, harps, angels. Some fools even think we become angels as if God would give us a demotion and make us exist in ways He never intended us to. But boy have I got some good news for you. Your body will die but your spirit can never die. And though your body dies yet it shall live. For a time your body will rot and decay. Cancer will eat at you until the worms do. A fatal crash will break you beyond repair, like

Humpty Dumpty. You will become old and cracked until your body betrays you and fails under its own weight.

But that is not the end. Your lungs may be filled with tumors but you will get new ones. Your body may be broken but it will be made whole. You may die old but you will be young again. Christ went into the cave a dead body but came out again a live body and we will too. We will be resurrected just like Him and live as body and soul. Not only will we die and be risen, so will the universe. The world will burn and die and there will be a new heavens and a new earth for us to live upon. We will eat and drink and sleep and play and laugh and work and sweat.

In the beginning Adam and Eve were given dominion and a charge. Subdue the wild. Make a garden of the earth. Care for the creation and enjoy it. Work with your hands and worship with your spirit. And those who follow Christ will return to this. We will be body and soul in perfection. We will make a garden of the world and sleep with no nightmares. We will worship and rejoice in the Lord. We will be whole.

You are dust. You come from a line stretching back eons. You are a link in a chain that connects and strengthens what comes next. You were born. You will die. But you are also breath. You will die, yet you shall live. This is what it means to be you.

Chapter 2
The World

All Your works with joy surround You,
Earth and heav'n reflect Your rays,
Stars and angels sing around You,
Center of unbroken praise;
Field and forest, vale and mountain,
Flow'ry meadow, flashing sea,
Chanting bird and flowing fountain
Call us to rejoice in Thee!
-from Joyful, Joyful We Adore Thee

Seasons

The world is young again in spring. The warming air stirs the resurrection life of budding trees and baby birds. I walk in my garden plot thinking and planning and sowing. Seeds for the future planted in the waiting ground. Corn, tomatoes, zucchini, spinach, and more all take their place in my plot. Reminders of life to come. All around my yard riots of daffodils burst up in rows, in clusters, in random spots. Whoever planted these in years past had no clear design or plan, just a sack of bulbs and a vision of an explosion of color and vibrant life to welcome the waking world. Reminders of beauty and glory.

The world turns and spring matures into summer. The birds grow up and get a job and move away from their parents. The seeds I planted many months ago begin showing the fruits of my weeding and watering and worrying. Reminders of growth and life. Summer is also the season of snakes. The strengthening sun bids them to come out of hiding and find their way into my yard. I don't mind that much. They have their place in this world just as I do. Dandelions begin to take root. Small sunbursts on my yard eventually giving way to the heads we love to kick and blow and that puppies love to eat. Life almost drips from the air in summer. Reminders of grace and gifts.

Fall is the most majestic of seasons. The ancient trees put on robes of many colors that would make Joseph blush. We've been enjoying early fruits but now the harvest begins in full. The fields are ripe for harvest. Reminders of all we have to be thankful for. The air turns crisp and life begins to slow. With the majesty and bounty of maturity comes the foretaste of the coming end of it all. Reminders of the cycles of our lives.

Winter. The final season. The bleak and dreary end. Well, not all that bleak. There's Christmas and brilliant displays of glowing and twinkling lights. But despite that bright highlight, the garden is still empty and the dandelions are gone. The air turns clearer in the dead cold of winter. The earth slumbers but it turns my eyes upward to see the stars more crisply than at any other time of the year. Reminders of death and glory. But still the cold and the emptiness can eat and drain and depress. At least until the daffodils once again begin to peak their heads up through the ground. Reminders of the coming resurrection. The world will be young again in spring and so will I.

Farmers and Faith

I find that as I get older I have a greater and greater desire to work the earth. I try to grow as many of my own veggies and fruits as I can. We keep chickens and pigs in our backyard. My sister-in-law teasingly calls me Farmer Jake, but I don't mind. All the best old testament figures were farmers. Adam had the garden of Eden until he got the boot and had to start plowing up the wild. Abel kept sheep until his brother grew jealous and murderous. Noah grew grapes and drank of them too much. David was a shepherd before Saul chased him around Israel. Naboth had a vineyard until Jezebel wanted it and his life. On second thought maybe being a farmer isn't all that great. The track record is a little spotty.

Regardless of the correlation of farmers to unsavory events, the Old Testament is steeped in agrarian language and imagery everywhere you look. The people of old were farmers, shepherds, goat herders. They worked in the fields and were in and around nature every day. And when God speaks to them He uses language they would have understood. He doesn't say that He's as powerful as a nuclear bomb. He doesn't say He's as fast as a jet. He uses language that they and all other people throughout the world would understand. We see this use of agrarian language throughout the whole Bible. Two examples.

First Psalm 23:1-2, "The Lord is my shepherd; I shall not want. He makes me lie down in green pastures. He leads me beside still waters." The Lord is my shepherd. The psalmist uses this farming language to describe God Himself. God is a shepherd. The people would know shepherds or be shepherds and they would understand what that means. They would go out and shepherd or see shepherds and see their care and concern for their sheep. They would connect with this language. They would be familiar with the beauty and restfulness of green pastures and still waters.

A second example from Matthew 23:37, "O Jerusalem, Jerusalem, the city that kills the prophets and stones those who are sent to it! How often would I have gathered your children together as a hen gathers her brood under her wings, and you were not willing!"

Jesus says that He is like a mother hen that wants to gather her brood under her wings. He uses this language that anyone who has kept chickens would understand. They would have understood the care and concern that a mother hen has for her young ones. They would have seen the protective wings cover over the young chicks. They would know the danger and silliness of a chick refusing that protection as the hawk circles overhead.

These are just two examples of how God uses farming language to teach His people about himself, but farming language is just part of how God uses the world around us to teach His people about Himself. The entire world is used by God to explain Himself to His people. Farming just happens to be one of the chief areas where people and nature intersect. Over and over again, God uses this spinning ball of dirt, water, grass, chickens, puppies, snakes, and more to show who He is.

Hearing the World

"Holy, holy, holy is the Lord of hosts; the whole earth is full of his glory!" When the angels cry this in Isaiah 6:3, they aren't speaking in abstraction or prophecy or exaggeration. They are speaking present truth. The whole earth is full of his glory. It's not waiting for a future perfected state or there in some effectively meaningless metaphysical milieu. It's here now. It's shining through. It's *breaking* through. It's visible to see. See it in the trees, be they bare, green, or multi-hued. See it in the daffodils and dandelions. See it in the movement and cycles and bounty around. And yes, see it in the snakes and death and cold.

All of this world reflects who He is. He is speaking through it even now. Traditionally Christians have recognized two sources of what we'd call revelation. Two ways that God reveals His character and nature. Special revelation and general revelation. Special revelation is the Bible. It's specific, clear, words. General revelation is the world. It's the way God's nature is seen in the world. Paul knew this. Romans 1:19–20 "For what can be known about God is plain to them, because God has shown it to them. For his invisible attributes, namely, his eternal power and divine nature, have been clearly perceived, ever since the creation of the world, in the things that have been made." The things that have been made tell about God. What has been made? Open your door and behold what your Maker has made. Go see it, feel it, taste it, smell it, and *hear* it. Hear it in the way Psalm 19:1-4 speaks of the creation, "The heavens declare the glory of God, and the sky above proclaims his handiwork. Day to day pours out speech, and night to night reveals knowledge. There is no speech, nor are there words, whose voice is not heard. Their voice goes out through all the earth, and their words to the end of the world."

Have you ever heard a star? Have you ever listened to the moon? You've seen them I know, but do you have ears tuned to hear their voice, their words, their glorious songs of praise? Those with skeptical hearts and callused ears might mock me now. I can hear their thoughts, "Listen to the moon? What a bunch of hogwash. The moon is just a big rock in the sky. There's nothing special about it! It's not even that rare! We only have one. Jupiter has 79!" Hear Jesus on Palm Sunday as He was drawing near to His crucifixion and death in Jerusalem in Luke 19:36-40, And as he rode along, they spread their cloaks on the road. As he was drawing near—already on the way down the Mount of Olives—the whole multitude of his disciples began to rejoice and praise God with a loud voice for all the mighty works that they had seen, saying, "Blessed is the King who comes in the name of the Lord! Peace in heaven and glory in the highest!" And some of the Pharisees in the crowd said to him, "Teacher, rebuke your disciples." He answered, "I tell you, if these were silent, the very stones would cry out."

The very stones would cry out. Why? Certainly not because they were special stones or especially beautiful or great. Why would they cry out? Because their King was there. The radiance of the glory of God in human flesh rode over them and that glory required praise. Callused ears can't bear to hear *people* praise God much less stones, be they small and somewhere outside of Jerusalem or giant and orbiting our planet.

Tear the calluses away. Unstop your ears. Open your heart to the communication God is pouring out around you day by day, night by night. Not just in the sky but in all the things He has made. They are dying to tell you things about God. They are screaming truths. Not fully, not completely, but they're speaking nonetheless. The question is do you have ears to hear?

It's hard to hear when you're not even in the same room as someone. When we close ourselves off from the very presence of those who are communicating. What meaning could the glory of the stars or the tenacity of the dandelions convey when you never consider them? We want God to speak. We want God to tell us what to do. To split the heavens and thunder down a divine answer. Or maybe give us a still small whisper. We grow despondent when our prayers for guidance or answers go seemingly unheard and yet we don't even listen to His ways of speaking. We might read our bibles because we know we're supposed to, but when was the last time you read the world? Not like a pagan prophet looking for omens in the curve of empty bones or the dancing of fire, but like Solomon or Jesus.

Here were the two wisest men who had ever lived. Both were blessed with divine wisdom and guidance. What does Solomon say in Proverbs 6:6-9? "Go to the ant, O sluggard; consider her ways, and be wise. Without having any chief, officer, or ruler, she prepares her bread in summer and gathers her food in harvest. How long will you lie there, O sluggard? When will you arise from your sleep?"

What does the God-Man Jesus say in Matthew 6:25-26? "Therefore I tell you, do not be anxious about your life, what you will eat or what you will drink, nor about your body, what you will put on. Is not life more than food, and the body more than clothing? Look at the birds of the air: they neither sow nor reap nor gather into barns, and yet your heavenly Father feeds them. Are you not of more value than they?"

Go to the ant. Look at the birds. How do you think they came up with these beautiful and poignant insights? By hearing what God was speaking through the world. By considering and looking and learning of the things around them. Solomon watched the ants. He knew of their tireless work. He saw how God had made them and how their making reflected God's glory and spoke truth. Jesus looked at birds. He saw how His Father cared for them and heard what His Father was saying through that. These were men who listened to the world. But that requires being in the world. Being among the daffodils and birds and trees. And yes, being among the mosquitos and storms and poop and other unpleasant things. It might mean getting bites and rashes and scrapes. It might mean getting dirty and dusty.

When we think of the world we want things to be tidy. We want things clinical and sterile. How dare a snake take up residence in my lawn. Doesn't he know his place? How dare that puppy relieve herself there, doesn't she know about toilets? And don't even get me started on the bugs. Buzzing, biting, bloodsucking bugs. The world should either be beautiful scenery you can enjoy with a nice cup of coffee or locked away tightly in zoos or other places not our own.

But God didn't give us a world so easily compartmentalized despite our best efforts. We prune and cut and cement and develop. We think we're the masters of our realms. Until we realize we're not. Until nature reminds us whose realm we're really in. If you want to know the boundary smashing nature of nature then just get puppies. They're so cute, so adorable, so uncomfortably real. We had a plumber come out to fix some issues once. He was a nice guy though he was very sweaty. He accidentally left our crawl space door open. Our two puppies didn't see a space that was forbidden to them. They didn't see a realm of men not accessible to lowly beasts like them. They saw a new play area and made quick work of some air conditioning ducts. Puppies cause troubles. Bugs bite. Snakes slither. Grass grows. Storms rage.

Watch the storm grow on the horizon. Black roiling clouds thick with rain and electricity. Feel your arm hair rise as the static in the air welcomes the coming rampage. Feel the wind ripping at your clothes. Feel the unbridled power and danger and beauty and command it, "Stop". You'd have more luck with that than puppies.

Now I'm not saying we should just all get back to nature and have no houses or cleanliness or hygiene. That we can't train animals or cut grass. What I'm saying is that one of the great lies we've been fed is that we're somehow above it all. That we exist in some kind of civilized bubble apart from the roiling biting chaotic beauty all around us.

You exist. We've seen that. But you don't exist in a vacuum. God has given you the greatest stage ever constructed to live out your part. A stage that somehow combines storms and puppies, waterfalls and poop, bugs and tomatoes all into a grand heavy mirror that shows us who He is.

Stand again on the edge of the storm. See the brilliant crack of light, a jagged line five times hotter than the surface of the sun. Wait a minute and feel the sound of air scarred by the heat. The thunder rolls, deep and thick. It moves through you and should move you. Feel it and *feel* it. Feel what it means in Psalm 29:3 that the God of glory thunders.

Go out in Spring as the earth renews and life returns. See the young calves leaving the barn for the first time. See the unmitigated joy in their prancing and dancing on the greening grass. See it and *see* it See what the Lord means when He says that on that day when He returns "You shall go out leaping like calves from the stall."

Get a beehive. Shepherd these tiny impossible creatures. So regimented, so efficient, so ridiculous. See them gather among the blooms and turn their labors into sweet honey. At the very least get some really good local honey. I'm not just being crunchy about this. It's amazing the differences you can taste in honey made near you. Taste the sweetness of the work of these flying, stinging, silly, buzzing bees and taste the words of Psalm 119:103, "How sweet are your words to my taste, sweeter than honey to my mouth!"

Go to a cookout. Smell the burning flesh of animals slain for you. Death and fire mingling to make a pleasing aroma like the levitical priests of old. Breathe in the scent of that sacrifice. Smell it and *smell* it. Smell what it means when Paul talks of Christ's death and taking on the fiery wrath of God in Ephesians 5:1–2 "walk in love, as Christ loved us and gave himself up for us, a fragrant offering and sacrifice to God."

Look up to the moon and stars and the sun and clouds. See the glory so lavishly painted above you day by day, night by night. Glory dripping from the sky. Glory that is almost excessive, almost inappropriately exorbitant. Listen to the moon. Hear it and *hear* it. Hear its speech revealing knowledge. Hear its voice throughout the earth.

The world is full of the glory of the Lord. It seeps from the air, the ground, the water, the plants, the animals, the clouds. It's all around for you to feel, taste, see, smell, and hear.

The Young Lions Roar

Once upon a time I bought eight little chicks. Each one was smaller than an apple and fuzzy with down. They chirped and peeped and ran around the little home I set up for them. They were adorable. They grew into majestic chickens. Beautiful and elegant. Feathers of white, orange, even some blue. I loved sitting and simply watching them sift through the fallen leaves looking for tasty insectoid treats. And then, disaster came in the form of a mink. A foot long monster covered in sleek brown fur, armed with sharp fangs and teeth and a hunger for death. Chicken death. I went to check on them before leaving for church and found every one of my sweet chickens dead. I cried as I gathered up their bodies. I cried as I dug their grave. I cried as I covered them with earth wet from rain, sweat, and tears. Lord, why?

Can you hunt prey for the mink? Or satisfy the appetite of its young? The earth is full of the glory of the Lord.

There are some who believe there was no animal death before the fall. I'm not so certain. I fully believe there was no human death. But when we look at all the teeth and claws and stingers, it seems to me that maybe the Lord made them that way for a reason. Regardless of whether or not animals were always meant to kill or not, surely they do now. And even in this God's glory shines through.

Hear from God's Word in Psalm 104:21 & 27-28, "The young lions roar for their prey, seeking their food from God. These all look to you, to give them their food in due season. When you give it to them, they gather it up; when you open your hand, they are filled with good things."

Do you know what lions eat? It ain't veggies. A meal for the lion is a tragedy for the gazelle. And yet, the lions seek their food from God. The Lord gives them their food and they are filled with good things. Good things. Gazelles slain and torn to pieces. Good things. What's more glorious? What's more beautiful? What's more worthy? What's more valuable? A lion or a gazelle? A mink or a chicken?

Seeing the glory of God in the world is easy when it's kittens and puppies and trees. It can even be easy in some of the biting and stinky and creeping things. But that's not all that's in the world. The world is full of leviathans and lions. And minks. What are these things meant to teach us about God? What praises do the young lions roar?

The people of Israel cried in the land of Egypt and God heard their cry and appeared to Moses in the burning bush.

He came with great news of freedom and deliverance, and yet Moses was afraid to look at God. Fear.

God came to Isaiah with a great mission and responsibility. He came in glory and Isaiah saw the Lord. And yet His response was to cry out. Woe is me! I am undone! Lamentation.

Jesus was divinity made flesh. He hid his full glory his whole time on earth except once. He took three of his closest friends up on a mountain and pulled back the curtain. He was transfigured and shone like the sun. The Father spoke from heaven saying this is my beloved Son with whom I am well pleased. Such beauty! Such majesty! Surely His friends would rejoice in this moment. Their response was to fall on their faces terrified. Distress.

The apostle John was on the isle of Patmos when Jesus appeared to him. Shining like the sun, eyes like fire. Surely the beloved disciple, the disciple whom Christ loved would be overjoyed to see his friend. John tells us, "When I saw him, I fell at his feet as though dead." Terror.

Anyone who gets close to God is filled with fear. Terror. Trembling. Lamentation. Distress. I imagine my chickens felt similarly seeing the mink. What's the point of pointy bits? Of teeth and claws and stingers and talons? In one sense their point is the point.

When we think of nature and who God is we're always in danger of cherry picking the things we like and ignoring the things we don't. We do the same thing with Scripture, but that's more obvious. Either way, we can be tempted to think of God as a doting senile grandfather. A little surly at times, sure, but generally good natured and harmless. But this idea of God is a golden calf. A false god.

For behold, I will bring a flood of waters upon the earth to destroy all flesh in which is the breath of life under heaven. Everything that is on the earth shall die.

-Genesis 6:17

The Lord is a man of war; the Lord is his name.

-Exodus 15:3

Bow your heavens, O Lord, and come down! Touch the mountains so that they smoke! Flash forth the lightning and scatter them; send out your arrows and rout them!

-Psalm 144:5–6

He also will drink the wine of God's wrath, poured full strength into the cup of His anger, and he will be tormented with fire and sulfur in the presence of the holy angels and in the presence of the Lamb.

-Revelation 14:10

God is a destroyer. God is a mighty warrior. God is an avenger. God is a conqueror. When the holy perfect God interacts with rebellious sinful humanity... Destruction. Death. Judgment. God is a lion among the gazelles, a mink among chickens. Now God is more than a destroyer. He loves and is kind and has mercy and is patient and is faithful to His promises. But He is not less.

C.S. Lewis understood this. The real one this time. He set about to write a story that would help teach children God's character and nature through a magical and fantastical story, *The Lion, the Witch, and the Wardrobe*. In this magical realm of talking beavers, fawns, and witches, Lewis has an animal character who is an allegory for Christ. What animal do you think he chose? An eagle, majestic and sleek? A dog, loyal and sweet? A lamb? That would certainly be biblical and appropriate. Christ was the lamb of God who took away the sin of the world. That would be a good choice!

No. Lewis chose for his Christ-figure Aslan to be a lion. There's a great line where the young children who have been transported into the magical land of Narnia learn of Aslan the King and learn that he is a lion. They are afraid and one of the children asks a very important question of one of the denizens of Narnia. Is Aslan safe?

Imagine standing face to face with a four hundred pound adult lion. A small mountain of muscle, claws, and teeth. No cage, no protection, just you and the lion. Is that safe? Would you feel safe? Is Aslan safe? Is God safe? Lewis knew the lesson of the mink well. He says through one of his characters, "Course he isn't safe. But he's good. He's the King, I tell you."

The young lions roar and the Lion of the Tribe of Judah roars back. And they are filled with good things.

Open Your Door

When we consider God's glory in the earth, every created thing is speaking to us and teaching us about its creator. We've talked of shepherds and hens, puppies and storms, bees and stars, minks and lions. But these are a small sample of everything out in the world. Behold, these are but the outskirts of his ways, and how small a whisper do we hear of Him! But the thunder of His power, who can understand? And what more shall I say? For the time would fail me to tell of God's glory in sunshine, food, crickets, whales, hippos, lizards, cacti, canyons, mountains, snow, rain, creeks, and more.

If we were to write down how every single created thing points to the glory of God and teaches us things about God then we would never finish writing. We cannot begin to plumb the depths of God's glory in the world in this one chapter and we have other topics to get to. Maybe one day I'll write a whole book on the things I've learned from the world, but that's another burp for another day.

For today, what I want you to feel is the weight of the world around you. Do you want to know God? Do you want to see who He is? Do you want to have a heart that is filled with wonder and praise? Then first open your Bible and second open your door. Get out into the world and listen.

Chapter 3
Love

The bride eyes not her garment,
but her dear bridegroom's face;
I will not gaze at glory,
but on my King of grace;
not at the crown he giveth,
but on his piercèd hand:
the Lamb is all the glory
of Emmanuel's land.
-from The Sands of Time are Sinking

Solomon in Mexico

I don't remember much of my wedding or even the days around it. Somewhere we have a video of the whole thing. My wife occasionally asks where it is and it seems my dim recollection of the wedding extends to the video too because for the life of me I can't remember where it is. That doesn't bother me though. I remember enough and I have a ring. A light weight around my finger constantly pulling and snagging and reminding and comforting.

One memory stands out from around this time though. We're on our honeymoon. A cruise around the gulf of Mexico. We've had many months of planning and frustration and anticipation and now finally, rest... and other things. We lay in hammocks on a golden beach in perfect weather. Sunlight plays through palm fronds. I look over and see her there. She's barely asleep, right on that magical edge where reality and dreams collide. How can I describe her in this remembered moment? Beautiful is too obvious and too physical. Lovely hits closer but it's still not right.

Ah, I have it. Ancient words, the first marriage vows when the world was young. Bone of my bone. Flesh of my flesh. She completes me, but not in a clichéd movie sense where I'm dumb and can fix cars and she's smart and needs her car fixed. No. This is deeper than personality or ability. She's a part of me I never knew I was missing until I did. Like never knowing you were meant to have two legs. Like never knowing what smell or taste or color was like. Like breathing for the first time in your life. And I'm desperate for breath in that moment.

I've never much enjoyed the beach. It's hot and sandy and the ocean holds terrifying leviathans and horrible dragons. But here now there's nowhere else I'd rather be than beside her. There's nowhere else I could be. My heart is full and the moment presses in on me, molding my heart, expanding and growing my capacity for love, my capacity for understanding love.

The wisest man in all the world gave a list of four things that were too wonderful and mysterious even for him to understand. Three things are too wonderful for me; four I do not understand: the way of an eagle in the sky, the way of a serpent on a rock, the way of a ship on the high seas, and the way of a man with a young woman. How does an eagle defeat the omnipresent downward pull of the earth?

Who can trace its path through the clouds and over lands unknown? How does a serpent with no legs move so quickly across the stone? Who can follow its trackless slippery path into the crevices of the rocks? How does a ship that weighs so much float so easily upon the water? Who can discern the passing of these marvels and follow in pursuit? How does a man come to love a woman and a woman love a man? Who can pick out the threads of love and understand the way two hearts are knit together?

I sit in Mexico and understand Solomon's confusion. How is this possible? I do not claim to have any answers to something that even Solomon could not grasp, but I do have my experience with love and the Scriptures. I can shed a little light onto this subject.

The Spark of Love

> Love's flashes are flashes of fire,
> the very flame of the Lord.
> - Song of Solomon 8:6

I first saw my wife at a mutual friend's birthday party. I remember entering my friend's apartment and seeing her on the couch. She was beautiful. My first thought was something along the lines of, Oh she's gorgeous. My second thought was, I'm sure she's married. I did a quick hand glance to check for the ring I was sure was there, but to my surprise she had no ring.

I don't remember much of the rest of the night. We didn't speak much, if at all. Dinner at a sushi restaurant, fun times with other friends, and eventually I leaned over to the guy sitting beside me and said, "Hey, what's that girl's name?" Rachel.

Was this love at first sight? Was this some kind of magical fairy tale moment? No. It was a small crush. A small hope. A thing almost certainly to never even start. It was mundane and everyday. But it was the start of something marvelous. It was the barest whisper of smoke from a spark that would become a fire.

If you've ever started a fire with flint and steel you know a lot about love already. You scrape and a multitude of sparks fly out towards the kindling. Most come to nothing. Bad conditions, incorrect timing, wrong place. Some catch a little but the small embers they make die away. Some might even start a flame but the wind picks up, they burn too quick, they sputter out. But every now and then a spark leaps and hits just right. And a small flame takes hold.

I actually met Rachel for the first time many days later at that same friend's apartment. Several of us came over to watch some movies. We joked and talked about Bruce Willis and aliens. I began to feel that spark taking hold. Over the next few months I began being around her more and more. And the more I got to know her the more that small sputtering flame grew. Each conversation, each joke, each memory was like a small twig carefully placed into the growing flame. You have to take these things slowly, you know. You can't rush a fire. If you try to do too much, try to throw on the big logs first you'll smother the fire.

I wasn't fully cognizant at the time of what was happening. I knew I kinda liked her and was maybe interested but before too long the fire made itself known. I knew that I had feelings for her and was interested in something more.

The Dancing Fire

> Many waters cannot quench love,
> neither can floods drown it.
> -Song of Solomon 8:7

Literature loves the adjective "dancing" for fire. Set a candle in the wind and you can see how appropriate the descriptor is and why it's so popular. Fire is blown about by the breeze easily. It moves to and fro even though it is tethered to its fuel. Too strong a wind and the tenuous connection between the flame and fuel is broken and it is gone.

I was aware of the growing feelings for Rachel I had and I decided to risk exposing that flame to the winds of chance. I sent her a message, an invite to lunch. Her response was not a fairy tale response. She said, "Is this a friend lunch or a date lunch? Because I'm not really interested in a date lunch." This was a blast of cold air from the west. This was a cup of many waters thrown on my little fire.

In another case, I might have huddled the fire close to my chest, hiding it from the wind, denying my intentions and hiding my feelings. I might have let the blast snuff it out and moved on to another spark, another fire. But something gripped me. I resolved to let the chips fall where they may and be honest. I told her the truth. I intended a date lunch but would happily take a friend lunch. We ate and talked and she explained some of why she wasn't interested in a relationship, but I let her know my feelings and explained that I wanted to continue to get to know her and wanted to date if and when she felt ready. I was waiting for her own fire to ignite.

We continued spending time together with other friends. Watching movies, going to dinners, laughing, joking, and eventually one night Rachel's own small flame was lit. She confessed that she had given it a lot of thought and had decided that she would like to go on a date with me. Here was a shot of pure 100% gasoline thrown on my heart. I wholeheartedly agreed and we set a time. Inside the flame of my love danced and I followed suit with a celebratory dance in my living room. I closed my eyes and bounded around to imaginary triumphant music. Moved by joy and excitement.

I hadn't realized my blinds were open. I learned later that Rachel saw the whole thing.

The Wedding Feast

> Eat, friends, drink, and be drunk with love!
> -Song of Solomon 5:1

Time would fail to tell of our dating and engagement. Suffice to say that we continued adding wood to the fire.

Continued getting to know each other and growing in love. I bought a ring, asked her father's blessing, and popped the question. We got married in St. Louis in January of 2016. As I've already said, I don't remember much. I remember Rachel getting overwhelmed by preparations and difficulties the day before. I remember stopping and dancing together. A moment of levity and ridiculousness to remind both of us of what really mattered. I remember sneaking outside to be alone with my pipe and my thoughts in the midst of the craziness. I remember my gathered family and friends. I remember my father reading Scripture. I remember singing songs of praise to God. I remember holding Rachel's hands and reciting vows. Most everything else is lost.

The day was a blur. The reception was more so. I can't remember the food we served or the songs we listened to, except the ones our DJ played despite our explicit forbiddance of them. But when I look back now almost six years later what I remember most of all is a general sense of being filled with love and joy and happiness. We and our friends and family sang and praised and prayed and ate and drank and celebrated the burning bonfire of love.

I was on a beach in Mexico when the reality of it all hit, but it hasn't stopped hitting. What seemed like a raging inferno all those years ago I now see as nothing more than a small kindling compared to the love we have today. Our wedding was just the start. There have been times when the storms of life have dimmed the blaze. There have been times when our own hearts have grown cold and lessened the fire somewhat. But on the whole it has grown more and more day by day.

What is Love?

What is love? Is love simply a deep affection? Is love service? Is love commitment? Is love sacrifice? I like the analogy given above and in the Song of Solomon. Love is a fire, the very fire of the Lord. And like a fire it requires fuel, care, commitment, it requires much in order to thrive. But it is not a greedy monster that hungers and is never full. Love gives more than it receives. It gives warmth, comfort, and utility. Love is deep affection, but it's also service. Love is an emotion, but it is also a commitment. Love is sweet, but it is also hard.

Love is multifaceted. We've focused on husband-wife love because that is the grandest and deepest human love, but there are other kinds of love. I love many things. I love my mother and father. I love my friends. I love my puppies. I love my garden. I love tobacco. I love bacon. I love cool mornings. I love storms.

How can we sum up love? What can we compare it to? Think of the things you love, both big and small. What do they do in your heart? When the bacon is sizzling, when the puppies are cuddling, when your wife is sleeping, how can you describe the feeling? Joy. Obviously. Contentment. Happiness. Commitment. Comfort. Esteem. Cherishing. Exalting. Maybe we could go deeper with a definition that may make you uncomfortable. In essence, love is worship.

Worship and Love

What does it mean to worship God? It means to cherish Him, to value Him, to praise Him, to obey Him, to follow Him, to glorify Him, and more. How would you sum up what God demands in His worship? What would a single sentence summary of all that worship does and could mean look like? Jesus has an answer. You shall love the Lord your God with all your heart and with all your soul and with all your mind. Jesus sums up worship and obedience as loving.

Worship we might say is love expressed. Love and worship go hand and hand. And so, what does it mean when we love other things? How is that not idolatry or wickedness? If love is a form of worship, should we then detach ourselves from loving other things? Should we be stoics or ascetics? Should we detach ourselves and refuse to love other things besides God or maybe just give in to our idolatry and not care? If I love bacon and love is worship, is bacon my god?

It certainly can be. Anything we love can become an idol. We don't worship and serve false gods because we hate them. We serve them because we love them. Whether it is money, food, success, or anything else, the things we love are gateways into idolatry. Consider Paul's words in Philippians 3:19 "Their end is destruction, their god is their belly, and they glory in their shame, with minds set on earthly things." It's unlikely that these people Paul is talking about simply woke up one morning and decided that their stomachs were actually the god of the universe that created all things and made them and deserves their worship and adoration. That would be insane.

Instead, what Paul is getting at is that these people worship their belly because they love to eat above all else. Food is their chief delight, their highest love. And that's what makes their belly their god. Their love leads to idolatry when that love eclipses their love for the True and Living God. Love is like a fire. It can warm and guide and sustain, and it can also burn when it is used inappropriately. It can destroy houses and lives and whole cities. Fire has a dangerous side when it is not used rightly.

So how do we love rightly? How do we love things without letting them become an idol? Do we have to resist a growing love and push it down when we feel that it is threatening to become an idol? Like pruning a blackberry bush that is growing too much or spraying water on a fire that is getting too wild. That's certainly a way to help with idolatry, but it's not sufficient on its own. There's a better way.

Imagine lighting two lighters. Two tiny flames of equal size. Now what would happen if you were to combine them? They would both grow greater as one fire. We can think of love and idolatry at times as though we have to control and master all these different loves to keep them from competing with our love for God, when God gives a better solution: bringing them all together, letting our love for various things join, support, and help grow our love for Him.

And so, I love bacon. I eat it and enjoy the salty flavor, the mildly crunchy texture, and the fulfilling nature of it. The fire of my love for bacon grows. But at the same time, I am reminded *through* this gift of bacon of the God who richly provides us with everything to enjoy. Who made bacon and all food. Who created pigs and made them have these muscles that develop and grow in such a way as to taste so wonderfully and satisfy so completely. I love our puppies. I love seeing their smiling faces and wagging tails. It fills me with joy to see them play and sleep and frolic. And through them I am reminded of the God who made puppies and His own joy and His own love. I am reminded of His own grace to me in giving me these puppies. And on and on and on. All of our loves are meant to remind us of God's goodness and worthiness and grow our fire of love for Him.

I relax on a beach in Mexico and look at my wife beside me. I lie in our bed and look at my wife beside me. I watch TV on the couch and look at my wife beside me. I sit in a chair in a hospital room and look at my wife beside me. I plant a row of beans and look at my wife beside me. I love her with every fiber of my being. Every piece of me is filled to bursting. She shines in my eyes. But it is not all her own light. She is a sunbeam. A gradient ray reaching down from the Sun of Righteousness above. I see her and love her, and yet I am inevitably drawn to the one to whom she is pointing towards. I see her kindness and know more of the kindness of God. I see her beauty and know more of the beauty of God. I see her faithfulness and know more of the faithfulness of God. I see her joy and know more the joy of the Lord. Over and over and over again.

To love is to worship. To love rightly is to worship God through the things you love. Love deeply and unashamedly.

Love and be loved. And in doing so you will find a fire that burns hotter than the sun. The very fire of the Lord.

Chapter 4
Church

Elect from every nation,
Yet one o'er all the earth,
Her charter of salvation,
One Lord, one faith, one birth;
One holy Name she blesses,
Partakes one holy food,
And to one hope she presses,
With every grace endued.
-from The Church's One Foundation

Too Much

A moment written fresh. Tired. Sore. After a weekend at youth retreat full of too much fun and noise. Returning to church just in time to take communion. Providence guided our wheels. Bread and wine. Body and blood.

Lunch is served. Men and women with gray hair and backs bent and broken from years of living and loving ask how we're feeling. Happy. Many games were played. There was sweet worship and teaching. Only minor injuries, no deaths. A success by any measure. Our only complaints are aches and sleepiness from hard "mattresses" and long days. We're not as young as we once were. Age has begun its work in us. We get laughs and assurances that it will get much worse. Death, that curse, met with cheerful eyes and chuckles. It seemed appropriate.

We load our plates with food from a folding table bulging under the weight of the potluck. There is no theme or organization. A riotous mix of side dishes, main dishes, two types of bread, and three types of salads. The chicken pot pie casserole from last time is gone so a baked ziti takes its place on my plate. I hope it's worthy of the space on my increasingly full plate. I can't try everything, there's too much. Too many people have labored over this meal. Too many people have made this work of art before me. Our church on a table. No picture or painting could ever do as much justice to these beautiful people as this table, held up by suspect legs and faith.

We sit and eat. A cup of sweet tea filled with too much ice joins the menagerie of offerings I chose. We talk to those around us about gardens and deer, peppers and babies. My wife tells a story of being tricked into eating horseradish. Another story is told about the dizzying effects of a deep breath of too much chopped horseradish. We laugh and eat. The ziti is very good. I might get seconds.

The meeting begins. Our pastor rises and begins talking about church business. He's talking with too much volume for where I am sitting. We don't have a sound system in this hall and many in the back have failing ears. We follow in the footsteps and instructions laid out two thousand years ago by electing a man to be an elder in the church. Votes are cast during our meal. It seems appropriate. After all, that's how the first elder was elected, on a beach amidst a meal of grilled fish. Feed my sheep. We are fed and fed and fed again. In word and sacrament and deed. He's elected unanimously.

We talk of church discipline and growth, vision and hopes. There is great praise given to God and the ladies who held a yard sale to pay for new hymnals. They raised too much in fact, we'll be getting new sound equipment too. To God be the glory great things He has done, he's given us hymnals without tape holding their bent and broken backs in place. One day he'll do the same to us.

A woman gets up to share a testimony of God's faithfulness in her life. Her voice and hands shake. Speaking in front of people is too much for her. But this is family. So she gets up and tells of her young daughter and the meningitis that ravaged her when she was still new to the world. Of the heart rending prognosis. Of the year-long days spent in the hospital. Of the visits and prayers. Of the pastor coming everyday. Of the nights that, in her fear and sorrow, she couldn't find words to speak to God or her infant daughter and could only sing her favorite hymn. To God be the glory great things He has done. The doctors had said she'd never talk or walk or show emotions. She assures us with happy tears that none of those things are true, especially the part about emotions. We all chuckle and praise.

A baby in the room begins crying. Her grandmother accidentally moved the purse the baby was playing with. I'm crying now too. I know I'm not alone because I can hear others sniffling. It's too much. Too much food. Too much love. Too much sorrow. Too much life. Too much grace. Too much to put into words.

The woman finishes her story. She's thankful for the church. She's no longer lonely now that she knows she's loved by God and these people, evidenced in prayers and visits, words and time, bread and wine, body and blood. I'm reeling now and crying too much. Others have stopped their sniffling but my eyes don't seem to have off buttons. I'm overwhelmed with the food and the love and the testimony and the grace and the great things God has done. I'm crying over new hymnals. It seems appropriate.

We sing the doxology together. No instruments. Just our unpolished voices joining together praising God from whom all these blessings have flowed. It is enough and too much. It is babies wailing and old women patiently repeating words for their deaf husbands. It is funny jokes and tragic stories. It is goofy slideshows and reports on church discipline. It is the words of life and financial graphs. It is ziti and pie. It is now and not yet. It is this cursed earth and the kingdom of God. It is bread and wine. It is His body and blood.

We leave, grateful to be on our way home after a long weekend. Grateful for rest. Grateful for our home. Grateful for the return to our mattress. My wife goes in to rest but I am restless. Too full from feeding and feeding and feeding again. Full of too much emotion. I need to digest.

I write about a moment while it was still fresh. But I am still tired and sore. So now, I think I'll go lie on the couch and put my feet up for a minute and take a nap. This morning was full but there's still tomorrow and the next and the next and then eternity. There will be more moments and meals. More small and great things. More ziti and pie. More tears and laughter. More bread and wine. More body and blood. After all, it's never really too much.

Feed My Sheep

On the night He was betrayed, after a supper of bread and wine, the Lord Jesus took water and a towel and washed his disciples feet. Peter, ever the zealot, refused to have Christ wash his feet. So great was his respect for Christ, he wouldn't allow Christ to stoop so low as to wash his feet. See Peter's great respect and honor for Jesus. How highly he thought of Christ. How much he esteemed and treasured Christ.

Upon hearing Christ say that unless He washed Peter's feet then Peter would have no part with Him, Peter went to the other extreme. Wash all of me! See Peter's great love and desire for Christ. How much he wanted to be Christ's and to be a part of Christ's people. Surely there was no better disciple, no one more dedicated to Christ!

When Christ tells Peter that Satan was going to sift him like wheat what was this loving and devoted servant's response? Lord, I am ready to go with you both to prison and to death! What devotion! What commitment! What complete and utter bullshit.

Christ knew Peter's true nature better than Peter. Peter, you *will* deny me. Not once. Not twice. But three full times. Before the sun comes up and the rooster crows on this very day that you have made such a grand profession and display of love and commitment and devotion.

And then the shepherd is taken and the sheep scatter. Peter finds himself around a charcoal fire with others as Christ is being put on trial and taken to his death. They recognize him as Christ's friend and ask if he was with this Jesus. I do not know him. I do not know him. I do not know him. And the rooster crows. Peter, the zealous, the respectful, the devoted, breaks down and weeps for His betrayal.

Fast forward the story a bit. Christ, risen from the grave, comes to His disciples on the shore of the sea just as the sun was rising and roosters in various towns and farms were crowing. The disciples were fishing from a boat and when they saw Him on the shore they started rowing back to the shore. Except Peter. He dove into the salty spray and swam straight to Christ. Ever the zealot. On the shore they found a meal of bread and fish prepared for them and they began to eat together once again gathered around a charcoal fire.

When they had finished breakfast, Jesus said to Simon Peter, "Simon, son of John, do you love me more than these?" He said to him, "Yes, Lord; you know that I love you." He said to him, "Feed my lambs." He said to him a second time, "Simon, son of John, do you love me?" He said to him, "Yes, Lord; you know that I love you." He said to him, "Tend my sheep." He said to him the third time, "Simon, son of John, do you love me?" Peter was grieved because he said to him the third time, "Do you love me?" and he said to him, "Lord, you know everything; you know that I love you." Jesus said to him, "Feed my sheep."
-John 21:15–18

Why was Peter grieved? Why did his eyes blur with tears when Christ asked him the third time if he loved Him? Why did his heart wrench at the questions? Two mornings. Two meals. Two gatherings. Two charcoal fires. Three denials. Three questions. Three times to remember and repent and grow. And three commands in light of that love. Feed my lambs. Tend my sheep. Feed my sheep.

This was a heavy moment for Peter. This was a moment that struck and sunk into him like a cannonball shot at point blank range with double powder. This was a moment he'd remember forever. A moment that would bring to mind his failure and Christ's forgiveness and his responsibility. A moment that would mold and shape him in ways beyond teaching. It would move him to lead, not as he had before with pride and zealotry but with humility and care. It would move to him to preach, not that the Kingdom would be given to Israel and her people but to Christ and people from all nations who follow him. It would move him to die, not from old age but crucified on a cross that he demanded be turned upside down because he knew he was not worthy to die in the same manner as His Lord.

It would move him to write in his first letter to the church dispersed in 1 Peter 5:1-11, "So I exhort the elders among you, as a fellow elder and a witness of the sufferings of Christ, as well as a partaker in the glory that is going to be revealed: shepherd the flock of God that is among you, exercising oversight, not under compulsion, but willingly, as God would have you; not for shameful gain, but eagerly; not domineering over those in your charge, but being examples to the flock. And when the chief Shepherd appears, you will receive the unfading crown of glory. Likewise, you who are younger, be subject to the elders. Clothe yourselves, all of you, with humility toward one another, for "God opposes the proud but gives grace to the humble."

Humble yourselves, therefore, under the mighty hand of God so that at the proper time he may exalt you, casting all your anxieties on him, because he cares for you. Be sober-minded; be watchful. Your adversary the devil prowls around like a roaring lion, seeking someone to devour. Resist him, firm in your faith, knowing that the same kinds of suffering are being experienced by your brotherhood throughout the world. And after you have suffered a little while, the God of all grace, who has called you to his eternal glory in Christ, will himself restore, confirm, strengthen, and establish you. To him be the dominion forever and ever. Amen."

What do you think ran through his mind when he encouraged elders to shepherd the sheep of their churches well? What does Peter know about feeding and tending Christ's lambs? What does Peter know of humbling yourself? Of recognizing our pride and unfounded zealotry and repenting of it? What does Peter know of God's care? Of having your worries and griefs and anxieties calmed by His love? What does Peter know of the power and ferocity of the one who demanded to sift him like wheat to show how much of his own bravado and devotion was nothing but empty husks? What does Peter know of both needing to be and being restored, confirmed, strengthened, and established by God's grace in Christ? Do you love me? Feed my sheep. Follow me.

Of Sheep and Shepherds

I love Peter's story here because it is in many ways your story and my story. A story of profession, sin, forgiveness, repentance, and growth. A cycle I've seen over and over again in my own life and you might have and will see in your own. Lord I will never. Lord I would never. Lord I will. And then betrayal and weeping. All our righteous professions are flimsy and weak rags that rip and tatter in the right circumstances. But even when we've been called on our own lies, Christ is waiting on the shore. Ready to welcome us and grow us.

You see, you and I are sheep. We may think of sheep as cute barnyard animals that everyone loves at petting zoos, but there's a reason connoisseurs of conspiracies use this offensive ovine designation for those who blindly follow the commands of the unseen and unsavory rulers of reality, whether they be big pharma or lizard people.

Sheep are stupid. They regularly get themselves stuck in literal and metaphorical tight spaces due to their insufficient intelligence.

Sheep are defenseless. No claws. Short teeth. Weak muscles. Slow feet. Sheep are the perfect prey for the lion and bear.

Sheep smell. Their thick coats gather all sorts of mud and muck and bugs and bodily fluids and give the sheep a memorable bouquet that makes working with them unpleasant.

Stupid, weak, unpleasant. That's you and me.

Oh but Jacob. I am not stupid. I have the highest GPA in my school! I've read so many books! I know so much! I scored so well on this test or that test! I have a bachelor's degree, a master's degree, a doctoral degree, years of experience in life and work! I have a high IQ! I would never betray you Christ. I am willing to go to prison and die for you.

The Lord may have given you many intellectual gifts. The Lord may have given you a mind to understand and know many wonderful things. But all you are is the sheep that has learned to unlock the gate. A slightly above average sheep, but still a stupid sheep.

Oh but Jacob, I am not weak. I have a strong body! Well tuned and taken care of. I have skills and ability! I am a war veteran, a prepper, a hard worker. I am strong! I would never betray you Christ. I am willing to go to prison and die for you.

The Lord may have given you a strong body. The Lord may have given you the ability and means to protect yourself to an extent. But all you are is the sheep that has learned how to headbutt other sheep. Your adversary the devil prowls around like a roaring lion, a dragon seeking to devour, and all your strength is as nothing before him. You are still a sheep.

Oh but Jacob, I am not unpleasant! I am loveable and sweet. I have many friends and get along with everyone. I have a high EQ. No one dislikes me, no one finds me offensive or annoying. Everyone loves me! I would never betray you Christ. I am willing to go to prison and die for you.

The Lord may have given you charisma and good relationships. The Lord may have blessed you with ease in friendships and family. But all you are is the goofy sheep or the sweet sheep that has learned to get along with other sheep. Your wool still stinks and is still brown around the rear. You are still a sheep.

I love Peter's story because it shows that despite all our intelligence and reason, despite all our strength and resolve, despite all our friendships and social skills, we are sheep. If Peter could go from great professions of devotion and sacrifice to denying His Lord and God three times in less than 8 hours what hope do we have? What hope do the sheep have in a world full of lions?

We are sheep. But we are Christ's sheep. We belong to Him. He is our shepherd. Being a shepherd was not a good occupation in ancient times. We idolize it in some sense today. The world grows cold and December rolls around and we get out little porcelain shepherds clothed in nicely painted tunics and place them out to display. I've yet to see a nativity scene shepherd with sheep scat painted ever so delicately on his boots or clothes. Maybe we should include a scented nativity scene. Grab the shepherds and take a deep whiff. Smell the body odor and the sheep odor.

These were men who spent their lives among these stupid animals day and night. They slept with them in the fields. They wrangled them when they got stuck in crevices or brambles. They fought off hungry lions with no guns. This was not a job your parents would want for you. This was not a respectable job. Shepherds were the laughingstock and social outcasts of polite society. No respectable person wanted to be a shepherd. No one with ability of mind or body or charisma aimed for this career track. This was the lowest of the low.

Listen to God incarnate. Lord and creator of heaven and earth. The high and holy one of Israel. He is above all in majesty and worth and honor says, "I am the good shepherd."

We are stupid. We are weak. We are unpleasant. And yet Christ came and lived among His sheep day and night. He got our scent on Him. He was maligned and an outcast. He fought off that roaring lion and dealt him a death blow. And now? Christ has gone and ascended into heaven. But he has not left us with nothing. He has not left His sheep without shepherds.

Life Among Sheep

I am one of those shepherds. I have been tested and tried by the local body of pastors in my denomination. Drilled on Origen, Finney, intinction, gnosticism, my sins, my struggles, and more. I have had men follow in the pattern of the apostles before us in the laying on of hands, signaling my admission into the office of elder. I am still weak, stupid, and smelly though. I still need the church.

Why is the church important? In an age of digital reality you can listen to sermons all day every day. You can have the greatest Bible commentaries and greatest insights on your screen in an instant. You can have incredible music and beautiful worship piped directly to you wherever you are. Why go to church and have to deal with sheep when it can just be you and the Lord?

The answer, like most important answers, is easy. We just may not like the answer. You need the church because you *need* the church. Despite our individualistic temptations and our potential aversions to the smell of other sheep, we are made to be a flock. There is nothing that can be substituted. There is nothing that can compare. There is nothing that can justify not committing to a local body of believers. At the end of the day, it can never be just you and the Lord, it must be y'all and the Lord.

It is through the church that the Lord works in our lives. It is where His word is preached. It is where His praises are sung. It is where His people gather. It is where we are sharpened like iron. It is where we learn from our fathers and mothers and brothers and sisters. It is where we are supported and prayed for. It is where we comfort others with the comfort we have received from the Lord. It is where we learn how to follow Him in suffering and distress. It is where we see His mighty works in the lives of others. It is where we rejoice with those who are rejoicing. It is where we weep with those who weep. It is where we learn of His glory and grace. It is where His Spirit is at work, convicting men of sin, strengthening faith, and encouraging righteousness. It is where we see the benefits of His redemption applied and sealed in the waters of baptism. It is where we see our Lord Jesus by faith in bread and wine.

It is where we belong. It is Christ's bride. It is Christ's body. It is Christ's house. We need the church because that is where our Lord is, in His temple. When we forsake the assembling together we forsake Him.

This is the easy answer, but it may not be an appreciated answer. It is easy to drift away from the body. Those people have hurt me. The preacher bores me. There are no people my age. There are no songs I like. I'm too tired, too busy, too shy. It is raining too hard for me to go. It is too beautiful for me to be inside. It's an inconvenience to me. I don't get what I want. I don't like what I get. What is the common denominator in all those answers? One of the major issues with how many people, maybe you included, view the church is a consumerist mindset. The church exists primarily to serve me and when MY wants, desires, preferences, time, or whatever isn't served well by the church, then I don't commit. We want an individualistic existence among the sheep. Where we are the star and the point. But the church is not meant to serve you. The church is meant to serve the flock of which you are meant to be a part.

The Lord is not content to give His people an individualistic existence. He intends for us to be connected with one another as a flock. You are a sheep and need help. You need help for your weakness and unpleasantness and stupidity. And God's provision for this weakness is as foolish and counterintuitive as everything He does is. His solution is a group of sheep, together. A flock. Under the truly good shepherd and His sheep undershepherds. Do not neglect the glorious place He has given to you. Instead, commit to a local church and be fed and protected. Yes, you will be offended. Yes, you will not get all the songs or programs or friends or wonderful things you think you deserve and want. Yes, it will require service and self-denial. But it is among the sheep where we find the Shepherd of our Souls and see His work and greatness proclaimed in His sanctuary. Do not forsake the assembling together of the saints as is the habit of some, but encourage your fellow sheep and all the more as we wait for our good shepherd to return.

Chapter 5
Fools

O come, thou Wisdom from on high,
and order all things far and nigh.
To us the path of knowledge show,
and cause us in thy ways to go.
-from O Come, O Come, Emmanuel

Fool

I stand in my kitchen working on a present for the second greatest woman in my life, my mother. Caring beyond comprehension. Kind beyond ken. Mother's Day is upon us and what gift can match such a magnanimous matriarch? Nothing money can buy. Something simple and earnest. A loaf of homemade bread, eggs, jam, and strawberries. The fruits of my efforts in my kitchen, garden, and coop. Such thought and such care in placing everything and making it right for the one to whom I in part owe my existence. Everything is just perfect. Except I forgot to put salt in the bread. What a fool.

I stand in front of my class of ninth graders teaching on the glories of the Old Testament. The grandeur of God's Law. The goodness of His promises. The greatness of His works. I reach a crescendo in my lesson pulling all the threads of covenants, Kingdom, and Christ together to drive home the point and try to help them see the light of the glory of God in the face of Jesus Christ! And a sudden and unexpected burp forces its way out of my mouth. What a fool.

I stand in my college room alone. The day has been long and my body is tired. The old bitter water sings its siren song to snare me. I feel it in my blood and broken flesh. The beast that promises life yet eats men alive. I know it will slay me and yet I take the cup and drink the poison. What a fool.

I stand in my yard looking at my garden. I have retreated to this patch of earth to hoe and plant and sweat. I am fleeing. Fleeing a dragon bigger and more terrible than any I've faced. Hoping that tired muscles and churned dirt will somehow keep him at bay. Tears join the sweat on the ground. I know where I should go for comfort and it is not the dust off the earth. And yet I do not run to the throne of grace for help in my time of need. I am angry. I am doubting. I am bitter. What a fool.

I stand in the pulpit in my church. Following in the divinely appointed instruction given to the church. I am preaching. Picking at a text from a book written millennia ago by uneducated fishermen, superstitious nomads, Bronze-age shepherds, biased religious zealots, and more untrustworthy types. Preaching about a God who is three and yet also one. About Christ who was fully God and fully man at once. About a God who died and a man who was raised from the dead. About a God who does not weigh our good deeds and bad deeds but instead asks only for faith. About a God who loves and dies for His enemies. What a fool.

Everyone is a Fool

Everyone you've ever met is a fool. That includes you, assuming you've actually met yourself. Everyone is a fool in big meaningful things and small silly things. There are no exceptions to this. There are only those who have come to terms with their own foolishness and thus become wise and those who stubbornly insist that they are wise and respectable and thus prove their own foolishness. It's an ironic thing but it's as true as the day is long.

Solomon, the wisest of all men wrote, "I said, 'I will be wise,' but it was far from me. That which has been is far off, and deep, very deep; who can find it out?" Here's the wisest man of all time, apart from the Lord Christ, and he says trying to be wise is impossible. If even Solomon in all his wisdom says, I am a fool, what hope do you or I have? None.

Job in his lament asks "Where shall wisdom be found? And where is the place of understanding?" You can't find wisdom in the depths of the sea. There is no mine for wisdom like there is for gold or iron. You can't buy it at the market. Its price is beyond pearls or topaz and yet it cannot be found anywhere on earth. Wisdom, wisdom, my kingdom for wisdom. And yet, where is it?

There are many who have claimed to have found it and yet have not. Self-important prophets of the all-powerful nothing and their edgy acolytes take to the internet and publishing houses to declare that wisdom is found in nothing. We come from nothing. Nothing has purpose. Nothing has meaning. Nothing was, is, and is to come.

Others hold that wisdom is the capitalist's king: Pragmatism. Pragmatism reigns from his throne on high and moves among men by his invisible hand. What works is what pleases him and let him be anathema who claims that the ends do not justify the means.

Still more hold to the humanist's creed. A royal cousin of Pragmatism who holds that what makes you happy is best. Reality is putty in your hands to mold to whatever might make your glands squish out those invisible happy chemicals. Truth is what you say. So say and slay queen. Be who you are and hold no mercy to those who oppose you.

And there are many many more. Those who believe they hold the key. That in their learning and reading and searching they have found the true answer to life, the universe, and everything and it is much more insidious and vile than simply 42.

Is there meaning in the world? Is there understanding anywhere? It is nowhere. It is wherever there is efficiency. It is wherever there is happiness. It is not a question worth asking. It is impossible to know. It is within you. It is whatever you want. It is...well, what is it? Where is wisdom found? How can you gain an understanding of life and suffering and everything? What is the right answer? Maybe a better question at this point is what is wisdom? What would it mean to be wise?

What is Wisdom?

How do you define wisdom? Surely it's more than knowledge. Satan knows much more than any of us and I hope we would not describe him as wise. But it necessarily includes knowledge of some kind, right? Solomon writes Proverbs explicitly so that the reader would know wisdom. And Proverbs is a big list of informative aphorisms meant to be read and known. So you have to *know* something. And yet, it is more than that.

Wisdom is understanding. It is to not only know information but to connect the dots between information and life and action and thought. It is knowledge applied to various situations. So there's a sense in which one could be extremely intelligent or knowledgable and yet have little wisdom. This is obvious in reality when we think about it.

I teach ninth graders and I see this all the time. A paper was due and the class knows that, thanks to the advent of cloud technology, I can and do check the edit history of the document. This is knowledge that I gave to them. This is information they have. And yet, I still have students who plagiarize when I can see them do it on the edit history! Fools! They have the knowledge and yet they do not allow that knowledge to influence how they behave and live.

Wisdom is allowing the knowledge we have to influence our lives. But that definition is further lacking because not all knowledge is true. I know for a fact that cottonmouths are friendly little creatures with no venom who love to be picked up and cuddled! That is true knowledge. Let's say that I act according to my knowledge. That is wisdom as defined so far. And yet on my way to the emergency room for the several venomous bites I inevitably receive, it would be right and true to call me a fool. So not only do you need to act on knowledge to be wise, the knowledge you have must be true and line up with reality. If you fail to act on knowledge you are a fool and if you act on false knowledge you are a fool.

Fools fools fools. All the way down.

And so, wisdom must be founded upon true knowledge and must result in action in line with that true knowledge. Which raises the question, where can one find true knowledge? And what is the definition of true knowledge? The prophet of nihilism and hedonism's philosopher could both claim to agree with this definition. In fact, all of the "wise" men and women above could sign off on this. And yet the fruit of their wisdom is poison. They act on what they believe to be true knowledge and yet it is not.

Where can Wisdom be Found?

And so, where are we to go to begin to gain the prerequisite true knowledge that will allow us to act in wisdom? Hear the Preacher, the wisest man, "The fear of the Lord is the beginning of wisdom." And again, "The Lord gives wisdom; from his mouth come knowledge and understanding."

The first step in being wise is to recognize that knowledge and wisdom are based in the Lord and not in ourselves. We are not competent nor sufficient to be wise on our own. We lack knowledge and the ability to act according to knowledge. How much do you know? How much knowledge have you amassed in your mental storehouses like so much grain and goods? Probably a good bit. But not enough to truly be wise. You might have a good deal of knowledge and true knowledge at that, but you cannot hold all things in your mind. Your tiny little wrinkly brain is finite and knowledge is unending.

Consider the weathermen of the news. Truly these are fools if there ever was a fool. With all the miracles of modern technology and centuries of metrological knowledge they cannot tell me for certain if it will rain next week or not. Now that's not to disparage weathermen. Most will admit that they do not know enough. To predict the weather accurately would require incredible knowledge of the humidity, winds, landscapes, temperature, cloud saturation, and thousands of more details that no one person could ever truly hold in their brain. And even then, it cannot be done with any certainty because these things are always changing and moving from day to day and minute to minute and there is no way to know how they will change until they do.

And yet, there is one whose way is in the whirlwind and storm. Who has cleft a channel for the torrents of rain and a way for the thunderbolt. Who brings rain on a land where no man is, on the desert in which there is no man. Who is the father of the rain and storm. Who has the knowledge the weathermen seek.

Job begins lamenting his tribulations and troubles. He endured difficult and terrible things. And his main contention, the main thing he wanted, was wisdom. He wanted to know why. He wanted to have understanding.

How could God do these things? We'll talk more about suffering in the next chapter but let's dwell for a moment here with Job. Where can we receive wisdom and understanding? Who is able to know all this and give guidance on how to live out that knowledge in wisdom? God answers Job's complaint out of the whirlwind and it seems...odd. He talks of the earth, the oceans, the weather, constellations, ravens, lions, ostriches, hawks, goats, Behemoth, Leviathan, and more. It's a weird response. Not what we'd hope for or expect.

Why didn't God just answer him? Why didn't God just tell him what he wanted to know? Why didn't He impart wisdom to Job about this situation? Because God was giving Job a greater gift. He was refocusing Job on the source of all knowledge and wisdom. God is telling Job, you are a fool. You know nothing. You don't know how to call rain or lightning. You don't know how to feed the lion and raven. You don't know how to birth the foals or make a horse. You can't make the wild ox obey you. You can't feed the eagles. You can't tickle the Behemoth. You can't play with the Leviathan. You are a fool.

But Job, you know Him who has all this knowledge and who can do all things. Trust in Him, fear Him, go to Him. And in that you may become wise. Not by knowing it all and professing your own knowledge and wisdom. But by confessing that you are a fool who needs wisdom from the Lord. And that's what Job does. He says, "I know that you can do all things, and that no purpose of yours can be thwarted. Therefore I have uttered what I did not understand, things too wonderful for me, which I did not know. I had heard of you by the hearing of the ear, but now my eye sees you; therefore I despise myself, and repent in dust and ashes."

Fools

Everyone you've ever met is a fool. There are no exceptions to this. There are only those who have come to terms with their own foolishness and seek the Lord as their source of wisdom and knowledge and thus become, and those who stubbornly insist that they are wise and respectable and thus prove their own foolishness.

The prophets and philosophers of the world claim to hold true knowledge that informs their wisdom and yet they are fools because the knowledge they have is faulty. The prophets of atheism claim that there is no God and yet, He is. King Pragmatism thunders that truth is whatever works and yet the Lord thunders louder that truth is what He says it is. The Hedonists clamor for their satisfaction and happiness, but God says that the point of life is not one's own desires and glandular stimulation, but obedience to and love for Him. The humanist says reality can be whatever you decide. Follow your heart. But the Lord says that He has set the foundations of the earth. He makes reality and He tells you what is true and right.

Those who find their knowledge and wisdom outside of the Word of God are fools. They are fools because they have rejected true truth and true wisdom. They have impoverished themselves and barred themselves from ever truly understanding life and reality. You do not need to take them seriously because they have not taken the Lord seriously. But you are a fool as well. You lack knowledge and understanding. You cannot know what you need on your own. You are like a blind man groping about for a knife in a pit of venomous cottonmouths. Insanely foolish. The only cure for foolishness is recognizing your own foolishness and going to the one who gives wisdom to the fools.

This is a heavy thing because it changes the way you view yourself and all others. There are no respectable people. You last of all. Do you feel pride in your vast expertise? Do you feel accomplished in your extensive learning and education? Do you look down on the simple and the fool? Do you trust in your own understanding? Do you rely on your own knowledge? What a fool. Join me in my foolishness. See and understand that you are little and know little. And in that gain wisdom and freedom "Let no one deceive himself. If anyone among you thinks that he is wise in this age, let him become a fool that he may become wise. For the wisdom of this world is folly with God. For it is written, "He catches the wise in their craftiness," and again, "The Lord knows the thoughts of the wise, that they are futile." So let no one boast in men." -1 Corinthians 3:18–21.

Do not boast in your own knowledge or wisdom. The Lord loves to make the "wise" look like fools in order to show that they are nothing next to him. He does this in big Jobian ways and in small but no less humbling ways. I begin thinking more of myself. I am something more than human. I am something powerful. Something grander. And the Lord sends a loud burp in a quiet room to shame me. To remind me that I am oh so human. I begin exalting my own knowledge and understanding. I know so very much. I have so many skills. And the Lord lets me forget to put salt in the bread. On and on and on it goes. The Lord loves to humble the prideful and remind us that we are fools.

The Lord is no stranger to fools. In many ways He is one Himself, at least from the perspective of the wise. We worship a God who sent His own son to die for the sins of fools who reject Him and hate Him. What kind of fool would bring pain, torture, and death to the one He loves most dearly for those who are His enemies? What kind of fool would put forth His son as a propitiation for the sins of fools? "For the word of the cross is folly to those who are perishing, but to us who are being saved it is the power of God. Where is the one who is wise? Where is the scribe? Where is the debater of this age? Has not God made foolish the wisdom of the world? For since, in the wisdom of God, the world did not know God through wisdom, it pleased God through the folly of what we preach to save those who believe. For Jews demand signs and Greeks seek wisdom, but we preach Christ crucified, a stumbling block to Jews and folly to Gentiles, but to those who are called, both Jews and Greeks, Christ the power of God and the wisdom of God. For the foolishness of God is wiser than men, and the weakness of God is stronger than men." -1 Corinthians 1:18–25

We serve a God who loves fools. Who acts like a fool according to the "wise" of this world. Who acts in unrespectable and illogical ways at times. Who gives us a gospel that is inherently foolish in order to upset the wisdom of pompous humanity. Why would you want to be wise in the eyes of those who hate this God? Why would you want to be respected by those who reject reality and truth? Why would you want to be seen as wise when God calls you to be seen as a fool?

This is a hard truth to grasp because it is a strong temptation to want to be wise. We want others to come to us for advice and counsel. We want to be sought after for our great learning and insight. We want to have answers and knowledge that we have found and compiled. We want to be treated seriously. And yet, the wisest men of all are those who recognize that being wise is far from them in themselves and yet near to them in the Lord.

Reject this desire. Reject the foolishness of the world. Embrace your own foolishness. Embrace the wisdom of God. Embrace your own inherent ridiculousness and find freedom to be a fool whose wisdom is found in Him who is wisdom and knowledge and truth.

Chapter 6

Suffering

Judge not the Lord by feeble sense,
But trust Him for his grace;
Behind a frowning providence
He hides a smiling face.
-from God Moves in a Mysterious Way

Nothing Else

The phone call came in
I heard it in your voice
Your tears and your fears
Nothing else is needed

You were on the porch
Sitting where I sit now
No words just a hug
Nothing else will comfort

We sit and we pray
Psalms and words and sayings
Built up like a raft
Nothing else to cling to

The day is a blur

Information and words
Meetings, calls, and naps
Nothing else is normal

We make jokes and smile
Fighting back the darkness
We cry, sigh, and breathe
Nothing else feels fitting

This dragon is strong
We feel our great weakness
We're given a sword
Nothing else can beat it

We will fight and strive
We will climb and slip back
We'll laugh and we'll cry
Nothing else is certain

A Picture

I keep a special picture on my phone. It's a picture of my wife at an Independence Day party. She's beautiful. She has her hair in a bun wrapped at the base with glow sticks. She looks off camera, towards an unseen explosion of fireworks. A few stray hairs tumble out of the bun, curly from the intense heat and humidity. Other than being gorgeous, there's no obvious reason why it's special or meaningful. Maybe that's part of why I like it. It's a normal picture at a normal event with normal things. A slice of time frozen in place back when things were normal. The last captured moment before the diagnosis and dread and doctors and disease. One last moment before our lives and bodies and hearts would forever be scarred by cancer.

Rachel received the call the Wednesday after the party. I rushed home. We sat on our back porch and prayed and read and...you read the poem, you know. The first few weeks were a blur of doctor visits, tests, new jargon, and both good and terrible news. We learned what triple negative meant, we learned about fish tests, we learned that we might never have biological children, we learned about neuropathy and other side effects that may or may not happen and may or may not be permanent.

I had thought the earliest weeks would be hardest, those days of confusion and uncertainty, not knowing if the cancer was contained or metastasized or what. Not knowing if this was a death sentence or not. And they were the hardest in one way. I had thought that the side effects would be the hardest, the loss of hair, energy, and all the other blessings of youth and the permanent damage of this healing poison to her body and our dreams and plans. And they were the hardest in one way. I had thought the ripples of all this into our lives would be the hardest. The loneliness I felt at church because the chemo hit so hard Rachel couldn't go, the space that sometimes grew between us as one or both of us failed each other and that failure was magnified by everything going on. Not seeing friends and family as often as we want or need due to the complications of disease and chemo. All the thousands of little ways our life had to adjust and move and settle around a little cherry tomato sized tumor. Something so small yet so unimaginably large. And it was the hardest in one way. But the truth was it was all hard.

On the very first day we began referring to the cancer as a dragon. An enemy to overcome. A frightful villain to slay. A dark and brooding evil in our life that threatened everything. And we knew that in life or death we would laugh in triumph over this dragon because our God is with us and He is in the business of saving little people and destroying great dragons. Even if it swallowed us, in the end He would keep us and stay with us and rip open its belly to pull us out. After all, He's been in the belly of the beast before Himself and knows the way out.

Since those first days there have been many days of tears. Many days of worry and disappointment and hardness. It's not been easy and it's not been all right.

I remember when she rang the bell at the cancer institute signaling to everyone in ear shot that she was finished with chemo. Joyous peals of freedom. In all honesty the bell seemed a little small. I wished they had giant church bells, the kind that require you to jump and use your full weight to pull the rope, the kind you can hear for miles. It seems more fitting.

I remember when she finished surgery and radiation. No bells this time. Just scars and a relief that there would be no more scalpels, no more pumping burning rays into her body.

For a while we were done with it and the cancer seemed to be defeated, but there was more. There were the continued side effects; scars and scorch marks from the fight that will never heal and never be set right. At least not in this age. There was the fatigue and difficulty of moving on from a fight that had worn us down to the bone and left our hearts threadbare. There was the worry and fear that the dragon would rear its head again or a vengeful cousin or lover hears of its demise and comes for revenge. After all, every good story deserves a sequel.

And our fears were realized. We thought we had dealt the death blow to the dragon. We thought its ire and fire were spent and the blood was cooling in its veins. But it was merely waiting to return with a vengeance. The cancer has returned and is terminal. We do not know what the future holds, only that it holds a funeral and tears. But then again, that's always the case for each and every one of us. We won a small battle and may even win this one, but in the end the war will be lost. It is inevitable.

It was lost eons ago when the first married couple encountered that first dragon, the Dragon, and listened to his honeyed lies and had their eyes opened to the reality of evil and darkness.

We will die.

We will suffer.

Suffering

Suffering is hard. The kind of hard that hits and gouges and scars. Suffering is a brawl in an alley behind a bar with broken bottles and fists wrapped around rolls of nickels. Suffering hurts. Suffering is real. Suffering takes on many forms. You can find it in the dark room of a young man struggling to find any joy or will to live. You can find it in the lonely heart of someone bereft of friends. You can find it in the awkward silence of a family learning to live without their mother. You can find it in the dull eyes of parents who've miscarried again. In waiting rooms and funeral homes. In churches and bars. In homes and parks. Suffering is everywhere if you look.

Suffering is a dragon. No, that's not exactly right. More accurately, suffering is the offspring of the Dragon. Suffering is the thrashing and gnashing of the Dragon. Suffering is a river billowing out of the lungs of the Dragon, seeking to overwhelm and drown all it can. Take your pick of analogies, the point is when there's suffering you can always find the Dragon nearby.

There was a man who suffered. He had paradise itself. Cool gardens and perfect peace. A lovely wife and all the world. And then, the Dragon. Destruction and curses. Toil, pain, death. Suffering.

There was a man who suffered. He had a lovely family, many possessions, health, a loving wife, all the marks of a great life. And then, the Dragon. Children crushed under a house. Possessions destroyed or stolen. His body a mass of sores and scabs. A wife cursing him and God. Suffering.

There was a man who suffered. He was the perfect man. Perfectly innocent. Perfectly holy. Everything you and I were ever meant to be and He did everything you and I were ever meant to do. And then, the Dragon. Stricken, smitten, and afflicted. A man of sorrows acquainted with grief. A cross, a crown, a spear, a tomb. Suffering.

Whence suffering? The Dragon. Easy question. Easy answer. Whence the Dragon? That's a good question, but not the best. We want harder questions. Why the Dragon? Why suffering? I know I've expressed my disdain for philosophy already, but let's borrow their language for a moment. I say, Why the Dragon? Philosophers say, the problem of evil. If God is good and omnipotent then He does not want evil or suffering to exist and has the power to make evil not exist. But evil and suffering do exist and so God is either not good, not powerful, or does not exist. Why did God allow the Dragon? Why the thrashing and gnashing? Why the cancer and death and loss and cross?

Philosophers couch it all in intellectual terms and fools memorize those axioms to wield like kindergartners who've found their parent's gun, but those who have felt tooth and claw know the reality of this argument. They may not know the axioms and logic of it, but they feel it. A deep keening pain. A real heart crying out, why?

Why was my wife diagnosed with aggressive breast cancer at 29 years old?

Why has it returned?

Why do we have to do this?

Why?

The Purpose of the Dragon

There are no easy answers. Easy answers are the retreat of fools. There are answers, but they are hard and uncomfortable. An answer big enough to answer such darkness is not easily swallowed. Like a pill bigger than your fist. You'll have to chew on it.

Why does suffering exist? If God is good and all powerful then why does suffering exist? Simple answer. He wants suffering to exist and the existence of suffering is better than no suffering. Simple answer, but a hard one. I'll let you sit with that while I go light my pipe. Okay. Ready for the next part? Why would suffering be better than no suffering? In what world would it be better to have pain and sorrow than not?

When Rachel was first diagnosed with cancer she felt fine. Nothing was wrong with her. She had a tumor but no pain, no suffering, no weakness. None of that came until we started chemo. Chemo sucked. Chemo wrecked her body and mind. It destroyed her hair, her energy, her strength, her will, her happiness, her youth, everything. And yet, chemo was good. This suffering was good. Not because of the suffering itself but because of what would come through the suffering.

Another analogy. One of my favorite artists of all time is Gustave Doré. Google some of his artwork. I'll wait. They're beautiful woodcuts of dark and light. But why does he use so much darkness? Doesn't he know that darkness is bad? Light is so much better. Let's just lighten all this up and get rid of all that nasty darkness. Of course that's foolishness. You lose all the beauty without the darkness. You don't see the point of the artwork. It's through the darkness that light has meaning and something beautiful is conveyed.

Why suffering? Because God was going to do something good through suffering. Because something beautiful would come from suffering. He uses suffering like chemo to defeat what's truly ailing us. He uses suffering like black ink to show something beautiful.

And again, there was a man who suffered. He was the perfect man. Perfectly innocent. Perfectly holy. Everything you and I were ever meant to be and He did everything you and I were ever meant to do. And then, the Dragon. Stricken, smitten, and afflicted. A man of sorrows acquainted with grief. A cross, a crown, a spear, a tomb. Suffering. And through that suffering, healing and beauty. Through that suffering, forgiveness and glory.

Suffering exists so that Christ could suffer on the cross and through that suffering defeat suffering once and for all. Evil exists to be taken up on that cross and triumphed over. Death exists for Christ to enter its belly and rip it apart from the inside, to lose its sting and victory. The dragon exists to be defeated. To have its head crushed underfoot in the victory of Christ through his suffering.

Every good story needs a dragon to kill. That's the answer to the question. Why does the dragon exist? To be destroyed. And then? Then the story gets really good.

"He will wipe away every tear from their eyes, and death shall be no more, neither shall there be mourning, nor crying, nor pain anymore, for the former things have passed away." -Revelation 21:4

How precious is this promise! How much joy these words bring! All because we have known death, mourning, crying, and pain. In a world without these we would have no way to grasp the preciousness of this promise. We'd have no gospel, no measure of God's love and faithfulness, no concept of good or evil. Suffering exists and it sucks. But God is not a God who allows purposeless suffering. He is not a God who revels in suffering. He is a God who uses suffering for good.

And this is a difficult truth. When you suffer, while in one sense it is the raging of the Dragon, it is also in another sense the Lord who is afflicting you. The Lord allows the dragon into your life to harm and maim. That's certainly the story of Job. Satan could not touch one head on the least of Job's camels until God said yes. Let alone Job's own head. Or his children's. There is no suffering that you go through that is not given to you by God.

"I am the Lord, and there is no other, besides me there is no God; I equip you, though you do not know me, that people may know, from the rising of the sun and from the west, that there is none besides me; I am the Lord, and there is no other. I form light and create darkness; I make well-being and create calamity; I am the Lord, who does all these things." Understand what is being said here in Isaiah 45:5-7. He's saying that He is in control. He is sovereign over goodness and suffering and He sends one and allows the other. Why? That people would know who He is. That His glory and nature would be seen in our lives and in reality.

What's hope without despair? What's love without loneliness? What's faith without doubt? What's the cross without sin? What's the gospel without suffering?

Why did my wife get cancer? Because through her suffering God was working things for our good and His glory. To help us understand the suffering of Christ more fully. To help us treasure God more deeply. To help us long for the day when the dragon is thrown into the lake of fire.

The Stewardship of Suffering

You have suffered, in big and small ways. You will continue to suffer. How will you react to suffering? If the Bible is true and suffering is given by God for good reasons then suffering is in many ways a gift to be stewarded. A blessing to be used well. How are we to rightly handle the suffering given to us?

When we encounter suffering in our lives we can be tempted to react in a few different ways. We can despair and give into the dragon. We can try to wrestle him down and crush his head ourselves. We can bring the full weight of human ingenuity and practicality against the dragon.

When we first received that dreaded diagnosis we felt all these temptations. I'd be lying if I said we didn't have to be strong. I'd be lying if I said we didn't rely and hope in the ingenuity of medicine and chemo. And I'd certainly be lying if I said there were no nights of despair where it felt like the river bellowed out of the dragon's mouth was drowning us and all we could do was weep.

But one of the greatest blessings of suffering is that it reminds us of our own insufficiencies and impotence. What good does despairing do in the face of the dragon? He will not take pity on you. Your tears are delightful to him. What good does your strength do in the face of the dragon? He is mighty and far stronger than you could ever dream of being. What good does your hope in human wisdom and ingenuity do? He's smarter and wiser than the sum of human intelligence. He is undefeatable by human strength. Suffering is inevitable, inescapable, and you are powerless in the face of the dragon who causes it. What a wonderful blessing to be reminded of these things! What a grace from God to have our self-pity, pride, and pragmatism shattered!

Suffering forces us to come face to face with the fact that we are not enough. It forces us to seek to respond in ways that steward this gift well. Instead of fighting on our own strength we are forced to trust and rely on the strength of the Lord. Instead of trusting in ingenuity and wisdom, we trust the gifts the Lord has given to men because they are His gifts to us. And instead of despairing and giving up, we despair but not as those who have no hope. Our hope in Christ sustains us through despair.

Suffer Well

But enough about Rachel and myself. Let's talk about you. You will suffer. Whether by cancer or loss or loneliness or a thousand different things. You will feel the teeth and claws and rage of the Dragon. This is a certainty. It may have come in part already. It will continue. If this is the case, then the question is not if you will suffer, but how you will suffer.

Frodo on the way through Moria felt the suffering of his situation deeply. Lost in a deep dark mine. Chased by orcs and wizards and monsters and evil unspeakable. Separated from the comfort and familiarity and peace of the Shire. He felt the claws of his own dragon and turned to advice from Gandalf, the wise and kind. Frodo said that he wished the Ring had never come to him and that none of this had ever happened.

How many times has Rachel said something similar? How many times have I? How many times have you? Probably many. If not verbally, certainly in our hearts we have felt this. Tolkien knew this feeling as a veteran of World War I, a time of unimaginable suffering and loss and horror. And what does Gandalf (and Tolkein through him) say in the face of Frodo's (and our) suffering? He tells Frodo that so do all who live to see such times, but that is not for them to decide. All we have to decide is what to do with the time that is given to us.

God has decided the suffering you are going through. It is His gift to you to steward well. You cannot choose what you will suffer, only how you will respond. And the way to respond is not despair, giving in to the Dragon. It is not relying on your own strength or the ingenuity of man. The response is to run to the Lord. To worship Him in the midst of suffering. To trust Him in the midst of evil.

This is the mindset of Job, who after losing his family, his wealth, his health, everything said, "Though God slay me, I will hope in him. The Lord has given and the Lord has taken away, Blessed be the name of the Lord."

This is the mindset of Habbakuk who not only said but sang, "Though the fig tree should not blossom, nor fruit be on the vines, the produce of the olive fail and the fields yield no food, the flock be cut off from the fold and there be no herd in the stalls, yet I will rejoice in the Lord; I will take joy in the God of my salvation. God, the Lord, is my strength"

This is the mindset of the Psalmist who said, "My soul thirsts for God, my tears have been my food day and night. Why are you cast down, O my soul, and why are you in turmoil within me? Hope in God; for I shall again praise him, my salvation and my God."

This is the mindset of the author of Hebrews who encouraged his audience with these words, "Jesus also suffered outside the gate in order to sanctify the people through his own blood. Therefore let us go to him outside the camp and bear the reproach he endured. For here we have no lasting city, but we seek the city that is to come."

And this is the mindset of our Lord Jesus Christ who as He approached the suffering of the cross and death, as He felt the Dragon's breath on His back that would soon be lashed, as He contemplated the claws of iron that would soon be piercing His feet and hands, told His disciples, "My soul is very sorrowful, even to death; remain here, and watch with me." And going a little farther he fell on his face and prayed, saying, "My Father, if it be possible, let this cup pass from me; nevertheless, not as I will, but as you will." Not as I will, not my desires, my wants, my ends. YOUR will be done. Even though it will cost me my life, even though I'm dying for people who hate You and rebel against You and run from You. Your will be done.

And what a glorious testimony these men are! For in these we see the true value of God to these men. What do you value? What do you love? What will you do when these things are taken from you in your suffering? Your health, your wealth, your friends, your joy, your family, your wife, your very life? Do you love these things more than God? Then you will hate God in your suffering. How could God take these things from me? But when you know the worth of the Lord and the goodness of Him, you will trust Him in these things and be a testimony to His goodness and worth.

But you will not do this perfectly. There will be times of despair. There will be times of trying to fight on your own strength. There will be times when you allow suffering to become your identity. There will be times when you will be stuck in the darkness. When you cannot follow in the example of these men. But in these times, recall to mind the goodness of the Lord. Trust in Him. Do not grow angry or bitter with Him. Do not follow the advice of Job's wife to curse God and die. Instead, look to the one who went to His own cup of suffering for you.

Suffering will come. The only choice you have is how you will respond to the dragon. My hope for you is to take this gift of God and steward it well. To feel the weight of the darkness and run to His arms for strength. To long for the day when He will wipe all your tears away. To learn and grow and join His Son in the fellowship of suffering. Suffering will come for you and me. When the Dragon rears His hateful horned head, my prayer for us is that we will suffer his rage well, trusting in the one who has already crushed that head and will finish the job in a little while.

May you suffer well.

Chapter 7

Sin

Let not conscience make you linger,
nor of fitness fondly dream;
all the fitness he requireth
is to feel your need of him.
Come, ye weary, heavy laden,
lost and ruined by the fall;
if you tarry till you're better,
you will never come at all.
-from Come, Ye Sinners, Poor and Needy

The Preterition of Sin

Most Christians at one point or another have tried to read through the Bible. New years and new hopes spur many to begin a yearly Bible reading plan. January arrives and resolutions are made. This year I'll get through the whole Bible. This year I'll read it all! Genesis goes pretty easily. We're familiar with the contours of the story and it's not too difficult. Exodus is also pretty easy, at least until the later chapters. The wheels usually fall off in Leviticus and Numbers. The confusing and seemingly incomprehensible law breaks whatever good intentions might have motivated us to read through the Scriptures.

This is unfortunate because I am convinced that few things would be more spiritually beneficial to Christians than to read all the Books of Moses. And I don't mean just skim through them. If by some cruel joke I was made Emperor of All Christians, my first Imperial Edict would be that all Christians must spend the entire next year reading, studying, preaching, and memorizing nothing but the Old Testament.

"But Jacob", I hear you say, "that's a little extreme! What about the gospels? What about the epistles? Don't other books of the Bible have things to teach us? And besides, that's the OLD Testament. Surely Christians should focus on the New Testament. On top of even that, those books are full of laws and stuff that don't even apply to Christians". If you feel any of these hypothetical objections or similar ones, allow me to explain my radical edict a bit.

One of the reasons I love the Old Testament is because it is unashamed in its diagnosis of the true problem of the world, sin. It might seem odd to include a whole chapter about sin. I have chapters on the glory of God in the world and love and existence and all these understandably big and heavy things. Why do I have a whole chapter about sin? Because sin is a weighty thing. Reading the Old Testament and seeing just how seriously God and the ancients took the problem of sin and the putridity of sin and the hope for a savior from sin molds you and weighs on you. This is a major issue with much of the world and Christendom today. Sin is light, sin is trivial, sin is neglected. But the Old Testament paints a different picture.

The Problem of Sin

Look at the sacrificial system. Stack up all the animals sacrificed in the tabernacle and temple. Gather up the blood spilled for sacrifice. Count up the time spent butchering and making these sacrifices. Add up all the monetary value of these sacrifices. What do you have?

Mountains of carcasses. Rivers of blood. Centuries of labor. Millions and millions of dollars of livestock wasted. All instituted by God. And not a bit of it could actually deal with even a single sin. It was all shadows and pictures. It was all ultimately useless in dealing with sin. And yet, sin is such a weighty matter, God says slaughter the lambs and bulls and more. Let the blood flow like waterfalls. Devote huge sections of your lives and livelihood to this task because what I'm teaching you through these things requires it.

How weighty is sin? The single smallest sin is heavier than the weight of the body and blood and effort and value of every animal ever sacrificed combined. Think about that for a moment. Think of how much your sin would require to be dealt with. You have many more sins than just one small sin. How much would you have to pay to random yourself? What could you possibly do under the weight of all your sin?

Not only is sin heavy but the punishment for sin is heavy in the Old Testament. Adam and Eve eat a little fruit and are cursed with death, toil, pain, exile, and creation itself broken. What they did was tiny. The world may have been filled with violence in Genesis 6, but surely there were children and others who weren't quite as bad. And yet, God sends a flood to wipe out the entire world outside of Noah and his family. Esau hadn't even done anything yet outside the womb and yet he was hated. Aaron's sons merely offered a kind of fire that God had not authorized. They didn't kill anyone. They didn't hurt anyone. And yet God consumed them with fire. Achan merely took some things that God had said should be destroyed. A cloak and some gold cost him his life, along with the lives of his wife and children who were in on it. Saul just offered a sacrifice with pure motives but still in rebellion and he had the kingdom taken from him and given to someone better than him. Uzzah just reached out to steady the ark so it wouldn't fall from the cart it was on and touch the mud. And God struck him dead. Even the smallest, well intentioned sin ends in seemingly insane punishment.

Why would God kill someone for things that are so small and inconsequential? We can understand death and punishment for larger things like murder and rape. But it seems a little excessive and capricious to kill for eating fruit, stealing some stuff that was going to be destroyed anyways, trying to steady the ark, and more. But again, the point God is making in the Old Testament is that there is no small sin. There is no inconsequential sin. Even the smallest sin is weighty enough to deserve death and conscious torment in hell forever and ever and ever and ever and ever and ever.

Why is sin such a big deal? Imagine you were to be incensed at me for writing something in this book. You find my address or church and decide to come pay me back for my offense. You walk up to me and slap me across the face. What will happen to you? Probably not much. You might get slapped back. You might get a little slap on the wrist from the law. But on the whole not very much will happen. Let's say you get upset at a governor's law and decide to go slap her. What would happen to you then? At the very least you will be arrested. You will likely face imprisonment and maybe even heavy charges. Let's say you get upset at the president and go slap him. You will definitely be going to prison and facing felony charges. That is if the Secret Service doesn't just kill you. As a person's importance and glory increases the penalty for crimes against them goes up as well. It's why the poor and needy are so easily oppressed and taken advantage of while the rich and powerful are much more protected.

Here's a question, how important is God in the grand scheme of things? How much glory does He have? He is infinitely important and infinitely glorious. A crime against Him, a rebellion against Him, a sin against Him strikes at the infinite and thus the penalty for such a crime is infinite.

The Old Testament shows that the problem of sin is that it is incurable and deserves infinite punishment. Every lie, every lustful thought, every covetous moment, every idol, no matter how big or small is impossible to pay for and earns you eternal punishment. But along with that, the weight of the problem of sin is meant to show us something else. If sin is this weighty, how weighty is the God against whom we sin?

The Putridity of Sin

I love pork. We have two pigs right now who are destined for the freezer. They spend their days eating hidden acorns and sleeping in the shade of the oak tree. Soon they will make excellent chops, sausage, bacon, and more. I imagine you enjoy bacon and other delicious things that pigs produce. Many wise people do. But in reading through the Law, one of the things we find is that the Israelites were forbidden from eating pork. In fact, they were forbidden from eating a lot of things. Shellfish, bats, camels, chameleons, and many more animals were labeled as unclean and eating them would cause one to become unclean as well.

This little facet of the law is a favorite of fools who wish to lampoon the supposed hypocrisy of Christians who enjoy some bacon-wrapped shrimp. "Don't you know the Bible doesn't allow that? You're a hypocrite." Spare me your idiocy. You neither know the Scriptures nor the power of God. My point here isn't to argue for why the Law is no longer binding on Christians. There are multitudes of volumes that deal with that topic. Instead, I want to focus on the why. Why does God introduce this concept of cleanness and uncleanness? The Law already teaches about sin and holiness and righteousness and wickedness. Why introduce this new category?

And why is this category so broad and seemingly arbitrary? Not only does eating certain animals make you unclean, there are other ways to become unclean. You can be made unclean by touching a carcass or dead body. You can be made unclean by contracting a skin disease. You can be made unclean by wearing a moldy or mildewy garment. You can be made unclean by your menstrual cycle. You can be made unclean by a discharge from your sexual organs. You can be made unclean for a variety of things and here's the rub, these things are not necessarily sinful or wrong. There's nothing wrong with burying your father or mother when they die and yet doing so would render you unclean. There's nothing inherently wrong with eating pork or shrimp. Pretty much all of the things that would make you unclean are morally neutral or even necessary. So what's the point? Why have this category?

There are a few possible explanations that have some merit and are probably true in part. One is the idea that these laws helped Israel develop a more hygienic and healthy culture. Many of the rites to become clean involved washing yourself or unclean items with water. Others involved isolating and quarantining the person or item, especially in regards to disease or moldy clothes. This created a healthier society as instead of handling dead, rotting carcasses and immediately eating a loaf of bread with your hands, you actually were supposed to wash. Those with leprosy or other diseases were identified and quarantined until they recovered or had to be sent away to avoid spreading it to others. This is a good explanation and true in part, but I don't think it fully explains the whole point of these laws. It gets at the practical but misses what God is actually teaching in these laws.

If God wanted a healthy society why not couch it in those terms? Why is there an added religious element to it? What God is doing in these laws is ingraining within His people a universal cultural disgust towards certain things that He can use to teach deeper things. We all have things that disgust us.

When I was younger I left a bowl of taco soup in a desk drawer by mistake. I wasn't supposed to have it in my room and heard my mom approaching. I quickly hid my shame in the desk drawer and my mom asked me to take care of a chore. I went and promptly forgot about the bowl. For several weeks. Slowly a smell began permeating my room. A revolting miasma that built and built. I searched for the culprit everywhere until I opened the desk drawer. The smell that hit me was indescribable. I watched as a bubble slowly popped on the surface of the soup. It was alive and it was disgusting. It was revolting. You could not have paid me any amount of money to take a bite of that soup. It might have bitten me back.

You have your own things that disgust you. Worms, fish, pickles, mustard, mayonnaise, poop, mold, boogers, burps, and more maybe. We each have things that cause us to recoil and gag. Things we consider unclean. Things that make us want to take a million showers after touching. But in that there is much to learn. God institutes these laws to ingrain this kind of revulsion into the Israelites. So that eating pork would be like taking a bite of that soup. So that touching a leper would be like sticking our hand into the toilet after a particularly explosive time on the throne. Disgusting, unthinkable, vomit-inducing.

And He does this so that when God's people start making offerings while tolerating sin in their midst God can say things like, "he who presents a grain offering, is like one who offers pig's blood." Disgusting. Unthinkable. Or so that He can say things like "You have all become like one who is unclean, and all your righteous deeds are like a polluted garment." Nasty. Repulsive. Or "Thus they became unclean by their acts, and played the whore in their deeds." Dirty. Revolting.

God uses the disgust generated by these unclean things as an analogy for His own response to sin. As much as we might feel disgust at whatever it might be, that is a pale shadow of God's own disgust. Sin makes Him gag. Our vileness makes him recoil. It is loathsome. It is gross. It is vomitous. Sin is disgusting in God's sight. Do you feel that? Think about that truly for a moment. Every little lie, every lustful thought, every moment of unrighteous anger, every small and big sin causes the God of the Universe to feel as disgusted at you as you would feel towards the most vile thing you can think of.

That's a good reminder and a good lesson, but it's not the only one. There are more treasures to be gleaned from these laws. Jesus was on His way down from a mountain with a great crowd following Him. And on his way down a leper came down. A man with a contagious and incurable skin disease that would rot the skin and cause pieces to drop off. You'd keep losing bits and pieces until you'd die. Lepers were understandably unclean. Touching them would make you unclean and potentially spread the illness to you. The leper approaches Christ and what does the leper say?

Surely he'd say, Lord heal me. Save me. Cure this illness. But no. The leper says, Lord, if you will, you can make me *clean.* You can make me clean. And Jesus surely would do this for him. He would say the word and the man would be healed. But He doesn't just say it. He stretched out His hand and touched him, saying, "I will; be *clean.*" The crowd was surely holding back their bile. There were surely audible gasps at this disgusting and depraved act. Jesus was going to make Himself unclean. Jesus was touching a leper. In essence Jesus takes up a spoon and digs right into the bowl of soup in my drawer. Vile. Repulsive. But let us read on. Immediately his leprosy left him and *he was made clean.*

This is one of those moments where the world is rocked and everything you thought you knew goes flying out the window. Centuries and centuries of generations of Israelites had lived under these cleanliness laws. They had been building a cultural understanding of the world over time that was as certain as physical laws. Gravity pulls downward. The sky is blue. Fire is hot. Touching a leper makes you unclean. Generations of people had been ingrained with this concept all building, in part, so that here on the side of this mountain the entire paradigm could be shattered and broken.

These Jews just started falling upwards. The sky turned neon green. Fire froze. Jesus touched this leper and the *leper was made clean.* As powerful and contagious as leprosy was, Jesus' own cleanness was more. He doesn't succumb to the taint of uncleanness, He spreads purity with every touch.

Sin is disgusting and revolting and unclean. Like a leper with all his fingers rotting off. But Jesus comes to not only deal with the leper but to deal with sin. To make us clean who are unclean in our acts, whose "righteous" deeds are like filthy unclean rags, whose worship is as good as pigs' blood. To deal with the shameful bowl of soup in the drawers of our hearts by eating it Himself. By becoming disgusting to His father and giving us His clean white robe. The laws of clean and unclean teach us about how God views sin and helps us understand more of what Christ did for us.

And this is just one example. This isn't even diving into the food laws and the other laws and unclean things that Jesus uses to teach about Himself, sin, eternity, and more. But if you don't read these books you don't get it. If you don't understand what God is doing with the putridity of sin you miss these glorious truths. So dig in. It's not bubbling yet.

The Pattern of a Savior

The Old Testament presents the problem of sin and the putridity of sin, but it does not leave us there. Many do not like the Old Testament because it feels like there's no gospel. It feels like there is no answer for sin. Where is Jesus? But read a little closer and see that the Old Testament is full of patterns of the savior to come. Jesus is everywhere in the Old Testament. God is showing what the solution to sin is going to look like from beginning to the end of the Old Testament.

There was a promise made by God. As our primordial parents felt the first pangs of death and toil and pain, God gave them a certainty. That serpent, that dragon, would have his head crushed by one of their descendants. His birth would be unique, only the seed of the woman. His work would be costly, the serpent would strike his heel. But His victory would be complete and the rebellion started by the serpent would be ended. Tell me, who does this wounded savior look like?

There was a man called by God who left all the comforts and familiarity of his home to go into a land as a stranger. A man full of faith and trust in God who did not waver. A man who was promised that through him blessing would come to all the earth. Tell me, who does Abraham look like in his faithfulness?

There was a man. King of Peace. King of Righteousness. Priest of the Most High God. He met the Man of Faith, our father Abraham, at a table in the wilderness. He blessed the faithful one and brought out bread and wine for a priestly meal. Tell me, who does this priest and king Melchizedek look like meeting his faithful one with bread and wine and peace and righteousness?

There was a man, a boy really. The Son of Promise whose birth was a miracle. His father's only begotten son whom the father loved. He was ordered up a mountain near where Jerusalem would be built and he was ordered to be offered up there as a sacrifice. He carried the wood he'd be sacrificed on up the mountain. He was silent as his father prepared him for sacrifice. He was to be given up so that the father's love would be shown and known. He was ready to die and to be resurrected. God stopped the knife but provided no lamb for sacrifice. Yet. Tell me, who does Isaac look like in his sacrifice?

There was a man who was despised and rejected by his people. Who should have ruled over them and been loved and praised, but instead suffered despite his innocence. But through his suffering he was raised to power at the right hand of the King in order to welcome, forgive, and save those who had rejected and betrayed him. Who told those who had hurt him, what you meant for evil God meant for good to save many. Tell me, who does Joseph look like in his power and forgiveness?

There was a man who left the comforts and riches of the King's house to go to his people. Who talked with God as a man speaks to his friend. Who interceded for the people to God. Who mediated a new covenant and brought a new law to the people. Who was faithful over all God's house and spoke the words God had given him. Tell me, who does Moses look like in his prophethood?

There was a man set apart to the Lord from the womb. Full of the Spirit in power and might. Who was betrayed by a traitor masquerading as a loved one. Who was sold for silver to his enemies. Who was bound, tortured, and mocked. Who in his final moments had his arms out to the left and right. Who prayed to his Lord with his final breath. Who by his death destroyed his enemies and freed his people from their slavery and oppression. Tell me, who does Samson look like with his body broken and arms outstretched?

There was a man who was king of Israel. A good shepherd and a man after God's own heart. Full of wisdom and strength. The hearts of the people were his. He won the battle against His people's greatest foe on his own for them.

He was seated on his throne in power with a sword in his fist. Who received a promise that one of his descendants would reign forever, make his people dwell securely, bring blessing to the earth, and seek after righteousness and peace. Tell me, who does David look like with his crown?

There was a place where Jacob slept and saw a vision. A ladder connecting heaven and earth. Bridging the gap between the divine and dust and bringing blessing from heaven to the earth. Tell me, Nathaniel, who does Jacob's Ladder look like?

There was a place where God and sinners could be reconciled and have peace. Where body and blood were broken and shed for harmony and fellowship between dust and divine. Where God's glory dwelt in the midst of His people. Where God's presence was seen and enjoyed. Where the garden was restored in part and things were beginning to be made right. Tell me, who does the tabernacle look like?

There was a serpent made from bronze. Pure and precious metal that was no serpent made to be a serpent, that ancient symbol of evil and sin. It was lifted up on a pole so that all who looked upon it in faith would be healed from the sting of the fiery serpents and be freed from death. Tell me, Nicodemus, who does this serpent look like?

There was a lamb that was perfect and without blemish or spot. A young male taken from the fold and made to live among the people of Israel. It dwelt in their home. It was beloved and cherished. It was slain. Its blood poured out. Its body was roasted with fire. Not one of its bones was broken. Its flesh was eaten as true food and its blood painted on the doorpost so that judgment would pass over and death would not darken the door of that house. Tell me, who does that paschal lamb look like?

There were sacrifices and prophecies and miracles and promises and prophets and kings and men and women and children and events and pronouncements and lions and lambs and trees and roses and so so so much more. Tell me, what is the Old Testament really about?

Jesus to the Pharisees, "You search the Scriptures because you think that in them you have eternal life; and *it is they that bear witness about me.*"

Sin is weighty. Let the cost and problem of sin sink into your bones. Let the putridity and vileness of sin sink into your bowels. Read the Old Testament and see how big it is, how pernicious it is, how insurmountable it is. Feel your sin crushing you like an ant under a world of granite. And then remember, you don't have to lift it. Someone else has promised to handle the weight of it all.

Chapter 8

Stories

Tis not to conflict now,
The sound of strife is o'er;
All tears are wiped away,
And sighs are heard no more.
'Tis to the banquet spread,
To join the festal throng;
Theirs is the shout of praise,
Theirs the eternal song.
The victor's crown they wear,
Crowned is their living head:
The wealth of Heaven is theirs,
His glory on them shed.
-from The Bridegroom Meets His Bride

My Story

I sit in the pews of Mountain Fork Primitive Baptist Church. My grandfather preaches with fire and unction but it is wasted on my young ears. At least for a season. It's wasted the same way the thousands of hidden acorns the squirrels forget are wasted. Hidden away and awaiting spring and new life.

I am young and do not want to sit in pews and listen to old voices singing about God and forgiveness and blood. I only want to be outside gathering all the fallen acorns and walnuts to hoard in my pockets and vex my mom during laundry. I listen to nothing but the birds outside.

Spin the world around a few times. I'm still young but less concerned with acorns. I sit in a biology class learning about our supposed ancestors. Apes, rats, fish, soup, nothing. The seed of my grandfather's preaching has never seen such a winter like the coldness of my heart. It has no place to catch root, no warmth, no rain. Just nothing. My heart is full of nothing.

A classmate raises his hand and protests what we're learning. He claims he believes God made all things. I laugh but inwardly I wish I was stupid enough to believe in God. Stupid enough to believe in purpose. Stupid enough to believe in beauty. Stupid enough to believe in something. I wish I was as foolish as him. But there's nothing.

A little further now. We're almost there. There. A girl, of course. Not Rachel, but important in her own way. My heart has been cold and hard but now for the first time there's something there. Like a vine growing in a crack in the wall. Striving, growing, breaking up the hard ground. Preparing me for something better and grander. Something I and every other child of dirt is made for.

She asks me to go to church. Another time and another me and I wouldn't have, but now I go. And slowly the hard rock begins being broken down. The girl moves on and so do I, but there's something still there. Maybe, just maybe, I was wrong. Maybe there is purpose and beauty and... Something. But I do not know what yet.

I sit in the pews of a church whose name I cannot remember. A summer camp for the church youth. Filled with songs and stories and fun. But in this moment there is none of that. We're given a card and a cross and told to list all the sins we can think that we've committed, write them down, and nail them to the cross. Another time and another me would've scoffed at the idea or thought of a respectable number to show I'd put the bare effort in, but this is different. In my heart there's a seed that's been waiting to grow. Winter and stone have kept it from sprouting but now at this moment, for the first time, the soil is right and the air is warming.

I began to write and write and write and write and write and write until the card was full front and back. I would've kept going but tears kept me from seeing what I was writing. What a sinner I am! What depth my depravity reaches! I am wholly unclean and awful. What hope have I? How can God love something like me? There's nothing to turn to.

But then, the cross. I took up my hammer and God took up my heart. And as I nailed the list to the cross the Lord breathed life into my heart for the first time. That seed that'd been waiting burst forth and for the first time in my life there was life.

Faith. Heavy and real. The gospel of a God who loved His enemies to death. Pressing and molding me into something new, someone new. Someone with something worth holding on to. Something worth dying for. Something worth living for. Something real.

I took my first true breath and laughed in joy.

God's Story

In the beginning God created the heavens and the earth. He spoke and reality leaped to obey. Stars, moons, storms, waterfalls, puppies, snakes, trees, iron, chickens, minks, lions, and more sprang into existence at His creative word. And to crown his creating work God took dust and breath and molded them into humanity. Man and wife, bone of my bone, flesh of my flesh. Hearts full of love and a whole earth to conquer. But then, the dragon. Rebellion and curses. Thorns, pain, toil, and death. And a promise. A seed of hope and redemption given to the newly cursed couple. Planted in their hearts and memories. Nourished with hope and faith. Someone would come to crush the head of that dragon. Someone would make things Right.

Millennia of life and death, faith and rebellion, promises and patterns pass and then the night broke and the sun rose on the first Christmas. At long last the seed had sprouted and all the centuries of hopes and dreams and faith were realized. Angels in the field appearing to smelly scat-stained shepherds. Heavenly choirs and riotous rejoicing. A savior is born. Rod of Jesse. Root of David. Prince of Peace. God with us. Divinity took on dust to destroy the dragon. He entered into the very world He created. He walked on rocks that sang His praises. He looked and saw the birds of the field. He touched people He formed. He hungered and thirsted and grew tired. He was tempted and tried. He grieved and wept. He loved and rejoiced. He was mistreated and misunderstood. He suffered.

He was taken into custody and beaten with whips made from cows He designed. He took up the cross made from trees He planted and watered and grew. He was nailed to the cross with nails taken from a vein of iron that He laced through the earth. He was crowned with thorns that He cursed the earth with. He was pierced by men He had made. His lungs gasped for air His words had formed. The maker of life died and the dragon roared in triumph.

What fool would go willingly to death? What fool would not use all the power he could muster to escape that cross? What fool would not call on God to destroy with fire and hail and all the plagues of Egypt those who were crucifying Him? A fool who knows that His foolishness is wisdom. A fool who knows that the cross is not defeat but victory.

The dragon roared in triumph as the Lamb of God died, but the Lion of the Tribe of Judah roared back in greater triumph. The cross was no mistake. His death was no victory for evil. His death was the death blow to evil.

How can sinners be made right before God? How can rebels have their crimes forgiven? How can the guilty be justified? How can God be just and merciful? Every sin you've ever committed cries out for your destruction. Every lie, every lustful thought, every selfish impulse, every prideful moment, every flash of anger, every rebellious decision, every day you've spent waging war against the King calls for you to be judged and thrown into the lake of fire where there is only gnashing of teeth, eternal agonizing torment, and no escape. That is justice for you and for me.

But God, being rich in mercy, did not leave us in that miserable estate. The cross was not a mistake and it was not merely physical torture, but rather on the cross, God takes our sins and rebellion and guilt and places them on Christ. He gave Him our punishment and gives His righteousness to those who trust in Him. Behold the Lamb of God who takes away the sin of the world.

And there's not only a cross, but a tomb. And not only a tomb, but an empty one. The giver of life was slain, but death had no power to keep Him. He endured death, that curse, and brought blessing. He went into the deep dark waters and parted them and paved a road through them with His own blood. He walked into the belly of the beast itself and ripped it apart from the inside. Not only was sin defeated, death itself was defeated. Though we die, yet we shall live. We shall never die. Let the reader understand. Death is a toothless enemy. It is a nap. It is a siesta. It is but a bright transition from a realm where joys decline to a realm of life eternal where God's endless glories shine. Christ rose from the dead and we will too in the True Spring. Just like the daffodils.

Sin is defeated. Death is defeated. And Satan, that ancient serpent, that tyrant, that *dragon*, is defeated. Through His death, Christ smashed the head of the dragon. The death blow was dealt to the one who brought death. And while he rages and gnashes and breathes out rivers of water seeking to drown all he can now, it's because he knows his time is short.

Christ has come to make things right. He began that work by defeating sin, Satan, and death and He continues that work today by ruling and reigning as King of Kings and Lord of Lords and will one day return to finish what He's started. The dead will rise and the world will be remade. No unclean thing will ever enter that place. No sorrow will ever darken its brightness. No dragon will rend and tear and rage.

Those who trust in Him will reign on the new earth as Adam and Eve were meant to originally. We will be made whole. We will be dust and breath forever. We will work and sweat and play and eat and laugh and drink and worship and rejoice. We will enter His courts with praises. We will sing a new song with fullness of joy. We will eat from the tree of life. We will build homes and live in them without worry. We will skip about as calves coming from their stalls after a very long and very cold winter. We will climb to the heights and plumb the depths of the earth.

We will taste the sweetness of the tree of life. We will see the Sun of Righteousness rising on the earth. We will hear the voice of myriads and myriads praising Him who sits on the Throne and the Lamb. We will feel the thunder of His presence. We will smell the aroma of life.

We will play with the Leviathans and tickle the Behemoths. We will tend to the puppies and the chickens and the lions and the minks and the tomatoes and the cucumbers and the daffodils. We will make the wilds and wastes bloom and blossom. We will make the whole earth a truly riotous and righteous garden.

And most gloriously of all, we will see His face and everything will be very very very *very* good forever.

The Weight of It All

I stand in the pulpit at my church trying to find some way to convey the wonder of all this. I stand in front of my 9th grade class at the Christian school I teach at trying to get them to understand and see the beauty of all this. I stand in front of my youth group trying to find some way, something that would cause them to weep and sing and shout for joy in light of this glorious gospel. I sit at my table outside writing a book, trying to put it all into words.

I know in all of these areas there are those who feel it. Those who feel the weight of the glory of God in the gospel of Christ pressing down and molding them and shaping them. I also know there are plenty who are like young me. Cold and stony hearts who hear nothing. They don't bother me as much as they used to. I'm a squirrel hiding acorns. One day, if the Lord wills, the time will be right. One day, if the Lord calls them, they'll feel the weight of it all.

This is the heaviest of all our topics. Everything else finds its source here. We exist as dust and breath. That is a weighty thing. To be physical and spiritual beings with beginnings and middles and ends. And we exist in this way for Christ to take up our dust and breathe our breath. The earth is full of the glory of God in trees and cows and iron and bread and wine and oil and thorns and hills. This is a weighty thing. God's glory shines in the world that is and all these things exist so that God's glory can be seen most clearly in how God uses His creation for His gospel. Creation is a stage for the gospel and the story of God's redemption.

The love I feel and you feel for bacon and dogs and trees and more exists and is weighty. The bonfire of love I have for Rachel is heavier still. And all of our loves exist to be as small trembling flames beside Christ's blazing inferno of love for His people. You are a sheep in a flock. The church God gives to His people is a weighty thing, and yet the church exists not for its own sake, not as a social club, not as a tool for self-improvement, but for Christ's worship. We are fools and it is weighty to consider how truly foolish we are. But never was there as big a fool as our God, sending His own Son to suffer and die for rebels.

Suffering will come. It is inevitable and terrible and such a great darkness and such an awful gift. The Dragon rages and rends. And this is a weighty thing, but suffering exists so that Christ could suffer and through His suffering destroy suffering. Sin is hugely weighty in its punishment and putridity. It is vile and severe. It is a weighty thing. And yet sin in all its enormity and power is declawed and defanged by the one who was typified and shown through all the patterns of the Old Testament. Everything we've talked about in this book meets here. The weight of this is the weight of it all.

Your Story

This is an incredibly short summary of God's story. To tell it in all its glory and splendor and depth would require book after book after book after book after book until the whole earth was filled with nothing but tomes and the weight of them all crushed the dirt into diamonds. This is the gospel that pressed into my heart that day 14 years ago. It molded me and changed me in ways that are beyond words. I was remade and reborn. I was myself and I was not. I was alive for the very first time in my life.

I don't know your story. I mean, maybe I do. I have to imagine that the audience for this little book is pretty localized around my own circles. So maybe I do know some of your story. Or maybe I don't. But God does. And you do too. You've learned about yourself in this book. You know who you are. You know where you are. You know who you should love. You know who's sheep you ought to be. You know you're a fool. You know your suffering. You know your sin. You know your own story. And I hope you know something of the life that Christ brings. The hope and forgiveness offered in the gospel story. I hope you've repented and trusted in Christ for salvation. I hope you've bowed before the King and followed Him.

If not, I invite you now to bow under this weight and let it change you. See that your existence is meant for this. You are dust and breath that is meant to live forever united together and with this King. The very rocks of this world all cry out the praise of this King. You breathe His air. You drink His water. You enjoy His world. You know His goodness because you've seen, felt, smelled, tasted, and heard it in millions of different ways though you have been calloused to it. The love you feel for others and others have for you is a pale shadow of the love you can know and experience in this King. You can have a truly good shepherd who gives you a home and a place to belong with His people. You can be a fool for Him. You can suffer well. You can have your sins forgiven. But most importantly and more primarily, you can have Him. You can have the King of all the Universe, the Lord of Hosts, the Living God, the Triune Majesty, the Father, the Son, and the Holy Spirit as your own. You are invited to leave your own ways and enter into His Kingdom this very day. It is a weighty thing but it is a glorious and real thing. Give up your nothing for something, better yet, for someone.

Take your true first breath, and laugh in joy.

Conclusion

The Smell

The Preacher sought to find words of delight,
and uprightly he wrote words of truth...
Of making many books there is no end,
and much study is a weariness of the flesh.
-Ecclesiastes 12:10, 12

The End of the Matter

You exist. You exist in a world full of beauty and terror and bugs and puppies. There's love and loss. There are faithful ones and fools and faithful fools. There's sin. There's a savior. These things eat at me. They press down upon me until I struggle to breathe. I've tried to relieve some of that pressure. To capture in writing some worthy thought or some worthy turn of phrase that will help myself and others. I've let out a whopper of a belch. And maybe you were impressed. Maybe the raucous and loud nature of it hit you right and you laughed or cried or were moved. But now comes the smell. The odorous miasma that turns any good burp into an offense, or maybe into something even more worthy of remembering.

All too often we're content to read and hear and be moved with no real impact. We nod our heads at the appropriate places, we say amen, we might even take some notes, but then it's over and nothing lasts. I don't want that for myself or you. These heavy things are not meant to be admired and moved on from. They're not meant to be dissected and discarded. They existed long before you or I and will continue to exist long after we return to dust. Some for eternity, some for shorter, but all longer than us. They're meant to press and shape and mold us into people who feel the weight of God through these things. To mark us and scar us. If you read this and have no scars, did you even listen?

My hands still aren't my father's, but I have more scars on my hands now. Every year I add to them. The pattern now is all too familiar. Whether working wood into furniture or fixing a broken lawnmower or other things. A slip, a pain, a bad word, a moment wondering how bad it is. And then comes the blood, the cleaning, the unhealthy pulling to see how deep it is, wondering if that's bone or just my imagination, and then the healing and the scar. Each year my hands look more like my father's. I've long since lost the jacket along with the poem, but I still think of both fondly. Each scar is a reminder of my chain of dust and the end of my own place in that chain.

I'm still adding to my garden. I just bought a taller fence to protect my tomatoes from ravenous puppies. I stop and listen to them, bright fruit singing praises by their very being. Our pigs are eating and growing. In a short while I'll take them on a little trip and return with plenty of bacon, ham, and sausage for us. I pause and give them a scratch on their back. They may be destined for the freezer but I am not calloused to their ridiculous mix of ugliness and cuteness, and after all, I'm destined for the dirt and I still want my back scratched.

I still carry a fire in my chest. I try to feed it well. Carefully stacking up memories and moments to feed the blaze of love for Rachel and through that the greater bonfire of my love for God.

I'm still a sheep and a shepherd. I'm still stupid, weak, and unpleasant at times, though I'm trying to set a good example for the flock.

I'm still a fool. No help for that.

Rachel's still fighting cancer. The battle with the dragon continues. But with every moment of suffering we are reminded that he has already been beaten. Just not by us.

I'm still a sinner with a savior.

The gospel is still there in every moment, every breath, every sigh, every laugh.

The Push of the Matter

What about you? You've read my words. You've heard my burp. Maybe you've felt the weight of these things. What will you do now? What life will you lead? This is the part you might not like because it requires a response. It requires work. It requires you to experience these things.

Will you continue on existing on your own terms? Whether by barely considering what that means or by playing the fool and listening to the honeyed lies of other fools that you are just a bag of chemicals? Will you live a life of meaning defined by your dust and breath?

Will you live a life of trying to separate yourself from creation? Shutting out the crying out of God's creation screaming the glory of God in rain and sun and sensible ways. Preferring a sterile and dull life over the beautiful stage God has given you?

Will you love and be loved? Will you use the loves you have, not as idolatrous strange fire with no purpose or direction, but as rays of sunlight shining down from the love of God above? Will you love God through the loves He has given you?

Will you be a part of the body? Will you see yourself as a weak, stupid, unpleasant sheep like Peter and myself? Will you recognize your need for the flock that God has given to you? Will you give up on your own consumeristic desire and commit to a church so that you can know God and be in His body with His people?

Will you admit you're a fool? Will you recognize that you are not wise or knowledgeable enough? Will you go to Him who has all knowledge and wisdom?

Will you steward your suffering well? Will you not give in to the dragon or darkness? Will you trust in the Lord though He takes your health, wealth, wife, or life? Will you cling to Him in His goodness, knowing He will make all suffering right?

Will you fight sin? Will you recognize the infinite danger of rebelling against an infinite God? Will you feel the foulness and vileness of sin? Will you see the pattern of a savior God provided for sin?

Will your story center on kneeling at the feet of King Jesus? Will you give up your nothing for someone? Will you join the story of the Risen King who has come to deal with sin and is coming again to save those who are eagerly waiting for Him? Will you take part in God's grand story?

These are my challenges to you, today, dear reader. They are not smart. They are not nuanced or eloquent. They are not philosophical. They are not easy. They are foolish because I am a fool and my God is a fool, at least in the world's eyes. They are blunt and unaccommodating because they are heavy and blunt things. They are real. They touch on the mud and blood of your life and they will change you. And that will be hard. To come to Jesus is to die to self. To commit to a church is to commit to people. To love is to be vulnerable and hurt. To do any of these things is to live a life you don't want to live because it's a life lived under the crushing weight of real realities.

It's the life of an ant trying to lift worlds of granite. It's a life of being molded by the heavy glory of God experienced and lived. It's to be overwhelmed and feel the pressure in your chest. I told you I needed relief and you will too. I told you I was overwhelmed and you will be too. These things are too big for you and my list is not exclusive. You will find things bigger and more glorious than you can imagine and you will feel the weight of that and it will hurt to have to change, to have to learn to accommodate this new burden.

But it is a glorious life because these things are glorious things. They are real and you are called to feel them and deal with them as a human made of dust and breath. This is your calling. This is your burden. This is your joy. Don't forsake it for plastic baubles and civilized lies. Drink deeply from this well. Write your own poems, sing your own songs, belch out your own books. I look forward to smelling them, I'm sure they'll be memorable and weighty.

I have sought to find words of delight, and uprightly write words of truth. Of making many books there is no end, and much study is a weariness of the flesh, but I pray that this meditation has been a good word. I leave you with one final poem. My deepest apologies, but I have to. You understand by now, I hope.

On Writing This Book

A Meditation, a Prayer, and a Benediction
(Or a Medipraydiction, if you will)

I sit and think and write
Striving, searching for words
To hit and cut and bite
Thousands of serifed swords

Words to delight and move
Words to describe and show
Words to define and prove
That you and I might grow

What words for one's own life?
What words for moon and tide?
What words for my sweet wife?

What words for Christ's dear bride?

How to describe the fool?
And the Dragon's dread rage?
And sin and its vile rule?
And more from page to page.

And pressing down most firm
The gospel, truth and grace
Christ, the God, made a worm
Bled and died in my place

Was this a waste of ink?
Shouting into the wind?
No grand noise and all stink?
Words I shouldn't have penned?

Of the writing of books
There is surely no end
Words flow like many brooks
Much study is no friend

But truth springs, not from me
But from Him whose Word lives
From the great One-in-Three
From Him who sweet grace gives

I hope and pray and pray
The weight of glory fills

The things I've tried to say
Only so, if He wills.

And so I ask in this rhyme
For Him to use this tome
And bless my ink and time
To bring many back home.

May He who made dust and breath
Made puppy, storm, and feather,
Made love that bests even death
And brought His sheep together

Who chose fools over the "wise"
Who crushed the Dragon's horned head
Who speaks truth while sin speaks lies
Who gives life and wine and bread

Who sent His Son to live and die
God in flesh, Immanuel
To breath his last and rise on high
Freeing us from death and Hell

May He, the King of all Kings
Grant you to feel the glory
Of these heavy and real things
And join in His grand story.

Amen and amen.

Epilogue

Haste thee on from grace to glory,
Armed by faith, and winged by prayer,
Heaven's eternal day's before thee,
God's own hand shall guide thee there.
Soon shall close thy earthly mission,
Swift shall pass thy pilgrim days;
Hope soon change to glad fruition,
Faith to sight, and prayer to praise.
-from Jesus, I My Cross Have Taken

The End of the Line

I began writing this book in late 2020. My wife, Rachel, had just been diagnosed with breast cancer and I needed a distraction that was productive and fun. It was also a bit of a catharsis and allowed me to process many things. I finished the chapter on suffering before we received the news in early 2022 that her cancer had returned and was terminal. I went back and rewrote that chapter and other parts of the book that touched on the issue of her cancer. In mid to late 2022, this book was essentially done. There is still some editing and some other final touches as I write this, but I have no plans for any major changes, though my life has undergone some pretty major changes since finishing this book.

You may have noticed, or not, that at the very beginning there was a dedication of this book, "In memory and honor of my beloved..." The bone of my bone and flesh of my flesh, Rachel died on March 1st, 2023 at around 8pm. She lost the battle, though my hope and her own is that we will win the war through Christ. I thought about reworking parts of the book after that happened. This book is written from the perspective of Rachel alive and it feels a little odd now reading it, knowing that if I were to write this currently it would look a little different.

Ultimately though, I decided against rewriting parts of this book. Rachel loved this book. She was not only a sweet encouragement in my writing of it but she was also my harshest critic. In many ways, whatever good this book does in the grand wide world can be traced to her and to me in almost equal measure. She inspired a great deal of it, our fight against cancer set the background for it all, she edited and critiqued and helped me sharpen it. She adored the work I had created and that she had helped finalize. For that reason, it feels almost like a desecration to stray too far from what I had already written. I want you to experience what I wrote as she did. And I fear that without her my writing will suffer fiercely, though perhaps it doesn't have far to fall.

No, instead I decided to include this epilogue enlightening you, dear reader, to the circumstances around the publishing of this book and Rachel's passing. I also wanted to share with you the homily I gave at her funeral, that you might know her and her savior better. Pray for me if you think of me. This road is hard and this burden is heavy. I have no doubt my sorrow is molding me in many glorious ways, but it does hurt and I miss her. But I shall see her again in the garden to come.

The Words of a Husband on the Death of His Wife

Pray for me to have the strength to do this. When Rachel and I first got the terminal diagnosis last year we obviously talked a lot about her death and funeral. She picked out the songs we've sung, but I had a request. I told her I wanted to give the homily and she said, Oh really? And I said, what am I not good enough for you? And she said no, I just wouldn't think you'd want to do that. And truth be told, I don't want to have to do it, but I told her, Rachel I'm a preacher and I want to preach. And I do want to preach today.

And the text I've chosen to preach on, briefly, is Joshua 23:14. Hear now the word of the Lord, "And now I am about to go the way of all the earth, and you know in your hearts and souls, all of you, that not one word has failed of all the good things that the Lord your God promised concerning you. All have come to pass for you; not one of them has failed." The grass withers and the flower falls but the word of the Lord abides forever.

Joshua is giving his last message to God's people. He knows his time is short. He sees death barreling towards him and he has one final address. One last word. And he discusses many things, but the crux of his message is here in verse 14. I'm going to die soon but God's promises have not failed.

The weird thing about this statement though is that they seemed to have failed. Or at least, they weren't all fulfilled when Joshua said this. God had promised to Abraham to bring blessing to the whole world through him and his line, and there'd been some gentile converts, but certainly not the whole world. God had promised to give them the whole land of Canaan and yet when Joshua dies while Canaan is mostly conquered there are plenty of pockets of resistance and whole cities and territories left that God hadn't dealt with. God had promised to make them into a holy nation and if you know anything about the people of Israel you that by and large they were not holy by any stretch of the imagination. They were complainers and grumblers and idolaters. No, when Joshua dies, it looks like many of the good things God has promised had failed. And I can imagine being at Joshua's funeral at Timnath-serah and thinking, God has failed.

But Joshua isn't just being naive or stupid in this verse. He knows what has been done and what is yet to be done. He knows what God has promised and how far those promises were from being fulfilled. But Joshua is making a point here to remind the people that God's faithfulness in the past is the evidence, the proof, the certainty of His faithfulness in the future. God had begun fulfilling His promises and nothing would stop Him. And because these promises are made by the unchanging omnipotent God of all the earth, they are as certain as if they were all already complete. There is no potentiality that they would not come to pass. In essence, they are so certain to come that it is right and proper to say that they already have come to pass.

And the proof of all this for the Israelites is what God has already done in beginning to fulfill His promises.

We might be tempted here today, in our sorrow and anguish, to feel or believe or even to say, God has failed. But the faith of Joshua is my faith, the faith of many of you, and it is Rachel's faith. God's promises have not failed and the proof for us this afternoon is His faithfulness in the past. For the Israelites they had bountiful evidence of God's faithfulness to His promises, the miracle of crossing the River Jordan, God bringing down the walls of Jericho, stopping the sun and fighting for them with hail and power, and more, but what about us today, here, in this house of mourning? Where are the grounds for our hope for God's promises to us?

There's another interesting verse that uses this same premise of speaking of a future certainty in the past tense grounded in God's faithfulness in the past. Romans 8:28–30, "And we know that for those who love God all things work together for good, for those who are called according to his purpose. For those whom he foreknew he also predestined to be conformed to the image of his Son, in order that he might be the firstborn among many brothers. And those whom he predestined he also called, and those whom he called he also justified, and those whom he justified he also glorified."

When Paul here speaks of being glorified he's referring to the future day when the dead in Christ shall rise in newness of life and receive glorified, perfect bodies that will never wear out, that will never fail, that will never fall prey to cancers or other diseases or injuries. And he speaks of this future event, this glorification, in the past tense. It's a certainty. So certain that it is right and proper to speak of it as already having happened. And Paul shows that the grounds for his certainty in this is seen in God's faithfulness in what has happened in the past. In this golden unbreakable chain that God has forged.

There's so much I want to say but I promised Rachel I'd keep it short. Though what she meant by short and what I mean by short may not fully align. I know right now it may feel foolish to say not one word has failed of all the good things that the Lord your God promised concerning Rachel. But the reality is that all have come to pass for you and for her; not one of them has failed. And the proof is what has come before.

God foreknew her. He has loved Rachel before the universe began and loves her now with a love that is deeper and brighter and warmer than the sum of all our loves for her. The candle I, you, all of us carry for her is as nothing besides the burning sun of God's love for her. Rachel knew this love and felt this love. She knew God as her loving Father and trusted in His love for her. And now she knows His love for her fully and immediately in His presence.

God foreknew her and He called her to Himself. From an early age Rachel heard the gospel call and God gave her faith. I've heard Rachel give her testimony many times and she always said that she couldn't put a time stamp on when God called her because it felt like she always knew Him. She was baptized into God's people as a covenant child. Bob and Susan raised her up in the nurture and admonition of the Lord, teaching her who God is and what

He has done for her, she was among God's people and had many wonderful teachers and friends who echoed the gospel call, and in her early youth God smiled upon her and she heard God's call to her and she believed. She did not have a crazy testimony with a huge moment of crisis but instead a gloriously mundane testimony of God's consistent faithfulness through ordinary means to call His children to Himself as He did with her and as He does with many.

God foreknew her, called her to Himself, and He justified her Rachel was by no means perfect and she'd be the first to tell you that. She was a sinner like you and like me. There are plenty of stories I could tell and many that Rachel probably wouldn't want me to. But I do remember one story of when Rachel was a young child. Bob was doing a project and Rachel picked up a little piece of some kind of insulation and was playing with it, but then Kristen wanted a turn playing with it and Bob told Rachel to give it to her. Rachel turned to Kristen and slowly tore it up before handing the pieces to Kristen, so smug and pleased with herself that she was obeying the letter of the law while still being able to rebel.

While she grew and matured, she had other moments of selfishness, bitterness, anger, and rebellion throughout her life. Not all were as innocuous as tearing up a piece of insulation. But her hope and her trust was not in her own righteousness or goodness or character. Rachel in the last year of her life was working through a legacy journal with prepared questions to help her leave a remembrance of herself and one of the questions in there asked, How do I describe myself and I want to read you what she wrote

"How do I describe myself? Redeemed by the precious blood of the Lamb. Bought with a price, sanctified, and justified in the name of Jesus Christ. Once enslaved by sin, saved by grace through faith: a gift from God, nothing to do with my own merit. When I am weak, I go to God. When I have sinned, he forgives me. I will be with him forever and ever."

She knew her sin, she knew she needed a savior, and she trusted in him. All her sin was accounted to Him and all His righteousness was accounted to her. By grace through faith God justified her in Christ and this was not of her own doing or works, but a gift from God fulfilling His promises to her.

God foreknew her, called her to Himself, justified her, and He predestined her to be conformed to the image of His Son. While Rachel was a sinner in need of a savior, she had that savior and sought to follow Him and model her life after Christ. Salvation has often been compared to a tree or vine. Christ himself made the illustration that He is the vine and we are the branches. Justification by faith in Christ is the root of salvation but the fruit is good works and holiness. And Rachel was a truly verdant and fruitful tree planted in the courts of the Lord. Her life was marked by Christ and everyone who knew her knew her savior by her kind spirit, her strong faith, her ardent love, her tender heart, her compassionate care and more.

And her being conformed to the image of Christ was evident even in these last days. When we discovered the cancer on her liver and knew she would die much much sooner than we had dared imagined, I remember being in the hospital by her bed holding her hand crying and praying with her. And she said to me that all of this, all of the cancer, all of the pain, all of the heartache and sorrow, all of it was worth it because she knew God would use it for good. She knew God would bring people to Himself through her suffering. God would encourage His people through her trials. God would use her pain, sorrow, and even death for good and glorious purposes. She knew He would glorify His name in and through her suffering and that was enough for her. He was enough for her.

Her mindset was the same as our savior, who when approaching His own death at about the same age as Rachel said in John 12:27–33, "Now is my soul troubled. And what shall I say? 'Father, save me from this hour'? But for this purpose I have come to this hour. Father, glorify your name. Now is the judgment of this world; now will the ruler of this world be cast out. And I, when I am lifted up from the earth, will draw all people to myself."

Christ's death had a good and divine purpose, the glory of God, Satan cast out and crushed underfoot, sinners like Rachel and me saved from sin and brought to God and given peace and forgiveness. Glory and goodness. And Rachel knew her own death was a good and glorious thing. For herself certainly, she knew that to die was gain for her since she'd be with Christ and that is far better than here. But also for others. She knew that God would use her death for good and glorious things that she would not see firsthand. That others would hear God's call through her story and come to know Him and trust Him more and find the salvation and peace that she knew and knows. In that and in innumerous other ways she was a picture and image of our blessed savior.

God foreknew her, he called her, he justified her, he predestined her to be conformed to the image of His Son. And it is a certainty, He will glorify her. So certain is this that we can rightly say with the Scripture, he has glorified her.

As she was on her deathbed, we had many visitors and friends. And I remember as one dear friend said goodbye Rachel held her hand and eyes and said, I will see you again. Rachel knew, we knew, she would not see her again here. But that's not what she meant and that wasn't her hope. Her hope, her certainty and mine is that we will see her again in glory.

Again from her legacy journal, "What I believe happens when we die: I don't know all the details. It is mysterious. But I know I will be with the Lord my God forever. I know my body will some day be perfected and there will be no more pain. He will wipe every tear from my eye. All will be well and as it was always meant to be."

This sums up all of God's good promises to Rachel, to me, to every believer in Christ. And this certainty is vouchsafed by the very nature and character of God who does not turn and forsake us, who does not change, whose compassions never fail, who remains the same yesterday, today, and forever. The infinite omnipotent God has promised and He will bring it to pass. Nothing can stand in His way. Nothing can thwart His purposes. Nothing will impede His promises, not even death itself. You can bank on it, you can trust in it,so much so as to consider it already fulfilled.

Those of us who trust in Christ for salvation will see her face again, and more gloriously we will see His face, and we will together with Rachel rejoice in His great faithfulness to us His children.

The bone of my bone, flesh of my flesh, my heart, my love, Rachel has gone the way of all the earth, but know in your hearts and souls, all of you, that not one word has failed of all the good things that the Lord our God promised concerning her or us. All have come to pass for her and us; not one of them has failed.

<u>Thanks</u>

Billy Hale for his dreams and desires and dust and breath.

Grandpa for his preaching and faithfulness and Grandma for her patience and care.

My father and mother for their wisdom, strength, love, and taco soup.

Bob and Susan for running late to church decades ago.

Adam for love and guidance and shepherding.

The Bookwyrms for encouraging me to tell stories and for unceasing and unfading friendship and prayers.

Florence and Louise for being (mostly) good girls and often falling asleep on my feet while writing.

My pipe for its companionship in tobacco.

The mink for teaching me about the terror of God.

The chickens and pigs and tomatoes for showing me the glory of God.

The Oh Hellos and others for the music and lyrics listened to while writing. Here's a playlist of songs on Spotify I listened to heavily throughout the writing process: https://tinyurl.com/5n94jme7

My moonshine, my love, my Rachel for nights of tears, days of joy, moments of laughter, and a life of love and praise and wonder.

My King for the life and Life given to me, for puppies, storms, and minks, for grace, for love, for bread, for wine, for body, for blood, for suffering, for the crushing of the Dragon, for the garden to come. Come quickly, Lord Jesus.

About the Author

Rev. Jacob Hale is the Assistant Pastor of North Hills Church in Meridianville, AL. He also teaches 9th grade Old Testament and 11th/12th grade Apologetics at Westminster Christian Academy in Huntsville, AL. If you enjoyed this book you can follow him on Twitter at @Jacob_Hale or read more of his writing at the blog he shared with his wife, https://thoumybestthought.substack.com. When he's not preaching, teaching, or writing, Jacob enjoys smoking a pipe, trying to garden in stubborn Alabama red clay, and taking care of his rambunctious puppies, ravenous piglets, and resplendent chickens.

About Synod Press

Synod Press exists to publish books that promote a biblical worldview, are grounded in the historic Reformed faith, and are a delight to read. Our goal is to provide thoughtful, engaging, and relevant resources for Christians who seek to grow in their understanding of God's Word and their walk with Him. Check us out at synodpress.org or find us on Facebook.

www.ingramcontent.com/pod-product-compliance
Lightning Source LLC
Chambersburg PA
CBHW020938090426
42736CB00010B/1184